TO

7-1-63

The Ministry
of the Laity

THE MINISTRY OF THE LAITY

A Biblical Exposition

by Francis O. Ayres

THE WESTMINSTER PRESS
Philadelphia

1230811

To
My Wife
and Children

CONTENTS

FOREWORD

IN THE THIRTEEN YEARS I HAVE LIVED AT PARISHFIELD, I HAVE had the privilege of working with and learning from a great many people. Particularly in writing the second section of this book, I (with the others in the Parishfield Community) have been a member of a group of some sixty laymen, laywomen, and clergy who have worked together for more than three years to give expression to a Christian style of life. I hope many of them will recognize the contributions they have made to what is written here.

Anyone who knows Dietrich Bonhoeffer's writings will recognize my debt to him throughout the book. Beginning in comfort and ending on a gallows, his life in his last years was lived completely in this world. His writings are indispensable for an understanding of the Christian faith in our day. Although not as obvious, my debt to Hendrik Kraemer and Suzanne de Dietrich is almost as great. There are many others whom I might mention, especially men and women in the ecumenical movement. Among these is Jacques Ellul, whose contribution is obvious.

I would like to list all those who have helped Parishfield in many different ways over the years, but I will have to content myself by naming Gibson and Blair Winter, John and Eliza-

11

beth Musser, Richard and Beatrice Emrich. Without them,
the work reflected in this book would have been impossible.
Finally, I would like to thank the present members of the
Parishfield Community: Roger Barney, Jane Barney, Olive
Robinson. Not only did they arrange for me to have the time
to write but also they helped me with their suggestions and
criticisms. Roger Barney did his best to counteract my neglect
of English grammar and composition in school and college.
Our neighbor, Arlene DeWolf, typed a number of drafts of
the manuscript, working with my handwriting in a way that
indicates that the world has been denied a first-class hiero-
glyphist.

It is customary to end with a statement releasing everyone
but the author from responsibility. As much as lies within my
power, I now do so. However, all of the above are Christian
enough in their understanding to know they cannot be re-
lieved of all responsibility. Fortunately, they also know about
forgiveness for me and for themselves.

F.O.A.

INTRODUCTION

IN 1945 THE TERM "MINISTRY OF THE LAITY" WAS ALMOST UN-known in this country. The reason is not hard to find. The special circumstances through which the church in Europe had gained the insight were totally lacking over here. During the Nazi regime in Germany before the war and during the Nazi occupation of such countries as Holland after 1939, it became obvious that a church whose ministry was confined to what the clergy could do was hopelessly inadequate to the demands of the times.

In the first place, removing the clergy bodily by drafting them into the army and labor camps or by shipping them to concentration camps was an easy matter; a man who preached against the regime soon disappeared. Maintaining the institution and conducting the services then became the responsibility of laymen in those churches where the best and bravest clergymen had been in charge.

In the second place, and much more important, the real resistance against the Nazis had to take place within industry, within community and family life, and, in the end, within politics. This was true for Christians as for others. The Nazis did not object to people gathering for worship, let alone to an individual worshiping on his own. Preaching could be continued in such a way as to be unobjectionable. What the Nazis could not and would not tolerate was worship and preaching that resulted in action contrary to their wishes. For instance, some of the Dutch congregations aided and spoke for the Jews. One clergyman acting along these lines could accomplish very little and could quickly be removed. A hundred men and women acting in a hundred different places was a different matter entirely.

When the same countries faced the task of rebuilding after the war, some persons in the church had learned their lesson well. They saw that their faith would have little impact except as worship and preaching erupted into action by laymen in all areas of their lives. They saw, too, that the church itself would have to be reborn. The Nazis had brought out the best in the church; they had also revealed the worst. If laymen were to share in the ministry, not in some specialized job, but in their everyday lives, the church would have to rethink its nature and its task.

Things began to happen. During the occupation, the Church in World Movement was launched in Holland, aimed at the renewal of the church in general and, in particular, at the development of a ministry of the laity. Bad Boll, the first evangelical academy, was started in Germany in 1945 so that there could be a "conversation" between the church and the world. As something less than 5 per cent of the Germans were active in the church, the task was considerable. (Since that time the number of academies has increased to twenty, some in Eastern as well as in Western Germany.) At the end of 1946, in Switzerland, the World Council of Churches opened its Ecumenical Institute where the new insights could be developed, sharpened, and more widely realized. In 1948, the First Assembly of the World Council established a Department on the Laity to advance the work in all parts of the world.

The 1948 Assembly also wrote a short report that succinctly articulated the new insight. The report, called "The Significance of the Laity in the Church," reads, in part:

We are thinking of the lay member of the church not as a worker in the congregation, but as one living and working in the wider community. The question to be faced here is this: how can members of the church be enabled to see the bearing of their Christian faith on their life in their occupation? How can men and women who stand in the stress and problems of life be helped to see how they can obey *just there* the will of God? The fact is that in their occupations, whether they are doctors, lawyers, industrialists, farmers, steel workers, etc., they live in an increasingly secularized world. How to live and work there as Christians, as members of the church; how to give witness to their faith; how to think about the bearing of the Christian faith on the economic, social, political, and cultural realities and backgrounds, is for most of them a mystery. They are left to their own wits, which means that they largely live a life divided into two separate compartments resulting in frustration and the weakening of spiritual vitality. The church is for them not their source of strength and light, but a place for the satisfaction of a religious need isolated from the everyday realities of a modern world moulded by the effects of industrialism, technics, and standardization. This is the more disquieting from the Christian point of view because it is in flat contradiction of the fact that the Lord Jesus Christ claims the whole of life, and therefore, the Christian faith necessarily demands expression in all realms of life.

Fifteen years after the war, the ministry of the laity is widely acclaimed. Convention addresses, pamphlets, articles on the present state of the church, sermons calling for advance, special conferences—all have urged a development of the ministry of the laity. In the United States it has become a slogan of our time, one's enthusiasm for the concept a test of one's openness and mobility.

But with what a radically different meaning! The layman remains a second-class citizen, an assistant to the clergy, primarily a maintenance man in the institutional church. As in the spiritual, "everybody talkin' 'bout heav'n ain't goin' there." The church as a whole has remained unmoved.

By way of illustration, the opening paragraphs of an article from the *Ladies' Home Journal* may help:

Clayton Hewett, with the aid of his friend Bill Warren, was reaching a momentous decision. "Bill," he said, pounding his right fist into the palm of his left hand, "I can't go on working full time at the steel plant, and only giving part time to the church. I've got to give my life to God—to the church!"

In the kitchen of the red-brick parsonage, on that gray March evening five years ago, Nancy Warren and Grace Hewett chattered as they washed the Sunday-supper dishes. Upstairs, children laughed and romped. But the two men in the living room heard none of these domestic sounds, for they were deep in a discussion which was to change many lives.

"Help me, Bill," Clayton Hewett pleaded. "Couldn't I at least be a lay worker for the church?"

The Reverend William Warren, minister of the Protestant Episcopal Church of the Incarnation in Morrisville, Pennsylvania, looked thoughtfully at his friend and parishioner, the wiry young steelworker Clayton Hewett—passionate, argumentative, and deeply devoted to his church. Then he smiled.

"I've been praying for you to reach this decision, Clay," he said slowly. "But even now I don't think you're aiming high enough. Have you ever thought of entering the ministry?"

Consider the presuppositions of such an article. There are, it would seem, three levels in the church. At the top are the clergy. Lower down are professional lay workers, who give "full time" for the church. At the bottom are laymen. If a man wants to "give his *life* to God," he can do it only by being a clergyman or a professional lay worker. Men who "work full time in the steel plant" can give to God only that part of their life which is spent in "church work"—a very small portion of their time unless they neglect family, community, and even work. Women, in many denominations, are doomed to the lower levels.

Whether or not the author of the article reported word for

word the conversation between the two men, she has caught the thinking of the church. Those same presuppositions appear again and again in church periodicals as well as in popular magazines. A former lawyer reports: "To have found and known, and to find and know again and again the strength, the joy, the understanding, the forgiveness, the love, the gentleness, the generosity, and the many other marks peculiar to the Christian fellowship is what work in the church has meant. To know and find these marks as daily experiences are the intangible qualities of *full-time* church work. [Italics added.] These make the difference, a difference which brings a life that is rich and satisfying and worth all that one may be able to give of self and time and talent." Such experiences are, it would seem, denied a practicing lawyer except on Sunday morning and for whatever time he can spare from a busy week.

A man who had played a leading role in the development of aviation in this country, had commanded hundreds of flyers during the war and been retired as a brigadier general some years later, became a clergyman. "The layman can serve God and the church in many ways," he is quoted as saying, "but I felt I had to do more." The author of the biographical article adds, "Why did he decide to take up the way of the cross *on a full-time basis?*" [Italics added.] Apparently, aviation and the army are not fields in which one can give oneself fully to Christ, and commanding a bomber group flying missions over enemy territory is not the way of the cross, while being in charge of a parish is.

If questioned, each person quoted above might deny the interpretation given to what he says. That is just the point. As evidenced in these articles and in countless other statements, the church says one thing and does quite another. So ingrained are the old ways of thinking and acting that they are revealed time and again, often at the moment something else is trying to be said. The problem is not a new one. Chaucer described the relationship between priest and laymen: "If gold rust, what then will iron do?" Although most clergymen and most laymen know that the comparison is ridiculous, the misconception continues.

In the United States, for historical reasons, the problem presents itself in a peculiar way. For two hundred and fifty years the church was challenged to keep pace with the westward movement of population. Clergymen were unavailable in the numbers needed. The denominations that met the challenge were those which relied on laymen as "preachers." As a result, there has been a further confusion in this country between laymen and clergymen. More than in any of the older churches of the world, the American denominations see laymen as "preachers" and "witnesses"—in the narrow sense of preaching a sermon on Sunday morning or Wednesday evening and verbalizing the faith to people who know nothing of it. More than any other country in the world, the United States has developed "clericalized laymen."

What was once a historical necessity has become a grievous bondage. The lay ministry is seen primarily as a way of aiding and strengthening the ordained ministry of the church. The key word is "man power." When someone speaks of developing the man power of the church, he is usually thinking in terms of training laymen to conduct services, visit the sick, call on the lapsed or unconvinced, raise money and perform other tasks that go with maintaining the institutional life of the church, tasks that are viewed as primarily the work of the clergy, "who need help." The institutional life of the church does indeed have to be maintained, but such maintenance work is a minor part of the ministry of laymen. Admittedly, the clergy are overburdened; but relief will come only through rethinking the nature of the church and in the renewal of the church, rather than by trying to shore up the present framework of congregational life.

Some attempts to change the situation look impressive at first but on closer examination are seen to be dangerously misleading. One such attempt is to view tasks performed outside the institutional church as a man's or woman's "church work for the year." An officer in Kiwanis or the Parent-Teacher Association or a board member on a community chest agency is excused from working in the men's club or the women's guild while he or she does the other job. Although such a step seems to be in the right direction, it underlines the misconception that laymen's work is always something special, extracurricular, and part-time. It fails to take seriously the layman's ministry in work, home, or politics.

There are, of course, those who see clearly. After steel, aviation, military service, the law, and many other occupations have been dismissed as providing possibilities for a rich and satisfying Christian life, someone is bound to react. One layman writes to a church paper: "It is time that we realize that the parson and other badge wearers are outside much of the social, political, and economic forces of our multipower-centered society. To imply that this group is full-time to the exclusion of other members of the body is arrogance. . . . Such phrases have become part of the twentieth-century jargonese that tends to convey the notion that unless you have a collar or uniform you are really a second-rater in the religious club. . . . The world needs Christian lay people in the power centers more than the church needs badge wearers, the former being in no sense less 'full time' than the latter."

What has been accepted for more than six hundred years will not be lightly changed, certainly not by writing letters—or even books! The church urgently needs renewal. Too often, the need is seen and discussed simply in terms of organizations and programs. A layman begins to see the possibilities of a real ministry of the laity and decides to consult the parson and other men in his home church with a view to developing a plan that will soon produce such a ministry. A woman decides she will get the women's guild of which she is a member to make "The Ministry of the Laity" the study program for the next year. The clergyman who begins to see the possibilities just groans, for he realizes that what is required is no mere tinkering with the church's program, but a revolution in the church's life. Those who have worked for renewal know something of the cost it will demand.

Fortunately, the laity do not have to wait for the renewal of the church before they can begin a real ministry. It is not a question of *either* the renewal of the church *or* going on a journey of one's own. The renewal of the church will take place in and through the development of a ministry of the laity. A religion-as-usual point of view will block such a development. Changes are needed in the direction, structure, and daily life of congregations. The church faces inward, concerned with its own self-preservation. It strives for more and more members while neglecting the dimension of depth. It seeks "growth without evolution." As Max Picard says, "Where there is only the instant, there is no time to grow slowly and organically; there is only an enlargement in quantity. Things expand monstrously in quantity; no time is given to them so they can evolve to their manifold shapes."

Therefore the church, as a whole and in its component parts, needs to be challenged and helped to change its direction, structure, and daily life. An integral part of such change— just now the most important part—is a demonstration of the ministry of the laity and of the slow, organic growth necessary to achieve a real ministry. The first step in the renewal of the church is to encourage as many laymen as possible to see themselves as ministers. The gap between talk and action will continue until a vivid demonstration of a true ministry is given. If laymen delay until their whole congregation begins to move, nothing will happen. Some will find help and support from the clergy, some from other laymen, some from both. Others will have to rely for help and fellowship on those who are doing the Lord's work in the world without knowing it.

A few laymen have started; many more are needed. This book is an attempt to speak directly to what the ministry of the laity means for men and women in their daily lives. As such, it is offered as an encouragement to all those who want to develop a ministry and thus help renew the church.

Finally, a word on terminology. Many see the ministry of the laity as dividing clergy and laymen, pitting the one against the other; but except where clergy or laymen insist on the gold-iron theory, no conflict is implied or necessary. The word "laity" derives from a Greek word meaning "people" and, consequently, the people of God. Clergy as well as laymen belong to the laity. Although the specific illustrations in this book have to do with laymen, basically what is said applies with equal force to the clergy. Countless books have been written about the difference between clergy and laity. What is needed is a treatment of what the clergy *share* with laymen—but that is another book.

Just as the term "laity" seems to raise a conflict between clergy and laity, so it is thought to exclude women. Nothing could be farther from the truth. Laity includes men, women, boys and girls, young men and young women. In this book the term "layman" almost always is used to include women, just as the term "man" is used in the inclusive sense. The church, along with the culture of which it is too much a part, tends to fragment people into various and conflicting groups —men, women, youth, old age, married, unmarried, clergy, lay. The church needs to recover a sense of its wholeness, of being the people of God in which there is neither Jew nor Greek, neither slave nor free, neither male nor female—in other words, neither basic nor primary distinctions.

PART ONE

You Are a Minister

Chapter I

YOU ARE A MINISTER

YOU ARE A MINISTER OF CHRIST. IN ALL FAIRNESS, AN EXPOSITION
of the ministry of the laity has to begin with that statement.
If you are a baptized Christian, you are already a minister.
Whether you are ordained or not is immaterial. No matter how
you react, the statement remains true. You may be surprised,
alarmed, pleased, antagonized, suspicious, acquiescent, scorn-
ful, or enraged. Nevertheless, you are a minister of Christ.

To the statement, You are a minister of Christ, it is necessary to add, Therefore fulfill your ministry in him. One might
say to a slovenly girl: "You are a lovely person. You have been
given lovely hair, features, complexion, figure. Therefore make
yourself look lovely. Make evident what is in a sense already a
reality. In other words, wash up, straighten up, dress up."
Or one might say to a man who through fear, insecurity, laziness, or some other cause has never realized his capabilities,
"You are an able engineer: therefore perform like one." By
the same token, one can say to all who have been baptized
what Paul said to Archippus: "See that you fulfil the ministry
which you have received in the Lord" (Col. 4:17). Indeed, for
present purposes, the Biblical message may be summarized by
rephrasing Paul's words to Archippus: "You are a minister:
therefore fulfill your ministry."

It should be emphasized that in taking the brief message to Archippus as a summary of one facet of the Biblical message, the verse is not being used as a proof text. The Bible should not be used in such a way as to launch a flight of the imagination from one text. Nor is it permissible solemnly to state or stridently to shout, "The Bible says . . . ," reading some passage as though it would immediately mean the same to a housewife in Baton Rouge, a machine operator in Detroit, and a banker in New York. Even worse is to assume that the meaning of the words (as accurately as they can be translated) is as immediately apparent in the 1960's as it was to someone living in the year 60.

The Biblical message is always directed to a person or group of persons living at a particular moment in history and occupying a specific place in a family, community, and nation. If one would understand what a text is saying, one has to make every effort to understand what the writer or speaker was trying to say to the man or men to whom the words were addressed. Hearing many pious people talk about the Bible today, one gets a picture of a tall, hermetically sealed tube. At the top is God, at the bottom is the hearer; both are divorced from all contact with the world. A more violent falsification of the Biblical message would be hard to imagine. It is one more example of man's making God in his own image. God is concerned with persons, and men are persons to the extent to which they are involved in history.

Having said this, one has to admit that Archippus remains a nebulous figure. The only other time he is mentioned is in v. 2 of Paul's letter to Philemon. It is a measure of the clericalization of the church today that he is almost always thought of as an ordained clergyman. Although he had, no doubt, some special ministry and may have been an official, he may very well have been a layman. The important thing is Paul's silence on this point. Paul and the other writers of the New Testament, and many in the Old, simply take office-bearers for granted as necessary in the church. What they insist upon explicitly, insistently, and incessantly is that all men are ministers, equally important in the task that God has given to the church.

In this, as in many other instances, there is a unity in the Bible. Despite many contradictions, discrepancies, and polarities, one can speak of "the message of the Bible" or preface a statement with "The Bible holds . . . ," or even "The Bible says . . . ," as long as what one says reflects this unity. To paraphrase George Bernard Shaw's statement about the English: "There is nothing so good that you will not find it in the Bible, and nothing so bad that you will not find it in the Bible." On the cross, Jesus says, "Father, forgive them; for they know not what they do." After the contest on Mt. Carmel in which Elijah defeats the four hundred and fifty prophets of Baal, he has every single one of his opponents slaughtered by the brook of Kishon. Nevertheless, the message of the Bible is unmistakably forgiveness and not liquidation.

Paul's message to Archippus represents this unity in the Bible. Earlier in the same letter, Paul says to all the Colossians what he later says to Archippus: "As therefore you received Christ Jesus the Lord, so live in him, rooted and built up in him and established in the faith, just as you were taught, abounding in thanksgiving." Although no text can be used apart from its place in the whole and without relating it to the unity of the Bible, some texts seem to sum up and go to the heart of the Bible. Paul's line to Archippus is one of them.

You are a minister of Christ. The Bible, contrary to current opinion, spends almost no time in moralizing. According to the complete concordance of the Revised Standard Version, the word "must," in all its uses, appears only 203 times, and "ought" only 50—in almost 1300 pages! "And you show that you are a letter from Christ" (II Cor. 3:3), writes Paul. He does not say, "You ought to be a letter from Christ"; nor does he say, "O my dear friends, I beg you to become a letter from Christ"; nor does he try to force or to manipulate them in one way or another. He makes a simple statement: "You *are* a letter from Christ."

The church in Corinth was torn by factions. Some of the

members were as immoral as anyone outside. While some were faithful, others were proud, pious, hypocritical, dishonest, self-centered, ambitious. In short, there was little difference between the church in Corinth and the church today. This does not prevent Paul from writing with assurance: no matter how distorted the message may have become, the Corinthians are a letter from Christ, the only one for the other citizens of Corinth to read.

When the Bible is speaking of those who have already entered into a relationship with God—in the Old Testament through birth into the people of Israel, in the New Testament through baptism into the church—the emphasis is, first of all, on what they are. They are the salt of the earth, the light of the world, a colony of heaven, sons of light, sons of day, God's field, God's building, the body of Christ (and individually members of it), a chosen race, a royal priesthood, a holy nation. "You are not your own; you were bought with a price." (I Cor. 6:19–20.) "Already you are filled! Already you have become rich! . . . you have become kings!" (I Cor. 4:8.) A full list of such statements would fill many pages.

One can, of course, question the Bible. Although one has been baptized, one can reject what the Bible has to say about God and man. Nevertheless, if the Bible is the record of God's self-revelation, once a man has been baptized, he is a minister, and there is not a thing he can do about it. A man can change his citizenship or renounce it. He cannot change or renounce his ministry, for in baptism God has acted, and what God has done cannot be undone by man.

Who bears the responsibility for a man's failure to recognize and exercise his ministry is another question. Each person has to bear some responsibility himself. In varying degrees his family, his neighbors, his fellow church members, his pastor, and others bear responsibility. Certainly, the church does not make clear what the Bible goes to great lengths to emphasize: all baptized members are ministers. The church has concentrated on the ordained ministry and all but forgotten the lay ministry. However, when all this has been said, one arrives at the same point from which one started: if you are baptized, you are a minister of Christ.

Some people are impatient with all talk that does not have to do with what they call "the practical side." They keep interrupting any discussion of "You are . . ." with "Yes, yes, but what does one *do?*" They are like a very young man who appears at a personnel office expecting to be given a creative, absorbing, well-paid job—and right away! For the young man's sake as well as for the company's, the personnel officer will want to ask a few questions, such as, "Who are you?" and "What sort of person are you?" An impatient young man not only can get himself into a job for which he is not suited but also can pass up work for which he has real potentialities. As will be seen in Chapter V, each member of the church is given gifts with which to fulfill his ministry.

When the Bible says "You are . . . ," it is, of course, not considering the particular abilities or even the nature of various individuals. The Bible is interested in something immeasurably more important and basic. God has revealed what it means to be a man, and the Bible is the record of God's self-revelation. In the last analysis, the Bible is saying, "You are a man: therefore be a man." That is, God intends you to be a man; he has shown in Jesus Christ what it means to be a man; he has given you all you need to be a man: therefore be a man and not a beatnik, hipster, organization man, string-bean fashion model, pious parson, or some other caricature of a man. What a man *does* depends on what he thinks a man *is*.

Modern culture, reversing the Biblical process, says, "Fulfill yourself: thereby you will become." At a time when the voice of the huckster is heard everywhere in the land, the emphasis is: Be successful. Be wealthy. Be fashionable. Be equal. Be religious. Be secure. The list is endless. One must struggle and strive for a goal that is always in the future. Seldom is a man allowed to feel that he is a person. Not only are there innumerable answers to the question, What can man become?, but also most of the forces at work tend to depersonalize man, treating him as a thing among other things. For instance, there is the image of the successful executive. Outwardly it seems to offer much, for union officials, clergymen, doctors, and assembly-line workers all wear gray flannel suits or reasonable facsimiles thereof. Inwardly the image is seen to include ulcers, the creature of over-organization, a pocketbook responsive to the family television, and a carrot dangling well out of reach.

The best authors, playwrights, and artists have shown modern man what these false images have made of him. With ruthless honesty, they have exposed him as lonely, anxious, his life lacking meaning, endlessly seeking to prove his manhood in sexual exploits. Unfortunately, even the most talented of these authors, playwrights, and artists have little to put in the place of these images which they demonstrate to be illusions. They do point to the cause of the sickness, however. Man is lost until he has an image of himself that corresponds with reality. Like most of their contemporaries, they seem never to have paused long enough to hear what the Bible has to say about the nature of man.

Under the circumstances, it is tempting to drop the terms "minister" and "ministry." Man and minister seem to be at opposite poles from each other; moreover, everyone wants to be a man, while few want to be ministers. There are two reasons for sticking with "minister" and trying to give it fresh meaning. First, avoiding it leaves the clergy in full possession and dooms the church to the gold-iron theory; or, to use another metaphor, it houses the church in a split-level dwelling, the laymen in the cellar with a limited view and the clergy upstairs with all the comforts of home. Secondly, it abandons the clergy to a fate worse than death. If the task of the layman is to be a man, it is obvious that the clergyman has to be something else.

The ministry of the laity, including both laymen and clergy, is to be men, to help each other to be men, to help all people to be men. A beginning is made by recognizing that you are a minister, that you share in the task of ministry. There are two words here, "minister" and "ministry." It is important to differentiate between them before proceeding.

You are a minister of Christ. You have a share in the ministry of the church. The primary word is "ministry," for a minister is one who shares in the ministry. In earlier translations of the Bible, the words are used where "service," "to serve," and "servant" are now used. The ministry of the church is, therefore, the service of the church to the world; a minister is one who shares in that task. In order to clarify the nature and task of the church, Hendrik Kraemer has said that the church *is* ministry. The point is that the church does not first exist and then decide whether and how it will serve. *The church exists to serve the world* and has no being except as it is a servant.

If, then, the whole church exists to serve the world and does not exist except as a servant, any restriction of the ministry to a small fraction of the church's membership becomes ridiculous. The world consists of industry, business, politics, metropolitan complexes, schools, universities, family life, communications, and other areas of life. How can the clergy serve in all these areas when, in many cases, they have neither access to nor knowledge of them? The main reason the church obviously fails in being a servant—and, in this respect, fails in being the church—is that the ministry is seen as the prerogative of the clergy rather than of all the laity in all areas of their lives.

There are other synonyms for "ministry." "Work" is one of them. Bishop R. S. M. Emrich has made a useful distinction between church work and the work of the church. Church work has mainly to do with the "housekeeping" activities required by any institution; the work of the church is to be in the world as servant. Another synonym for "ministry" is the "self-expression" of the church. Even when the church concentrates on self-preservation it reveals what it is, in contrast to what God intends it to be. A third synonym is "task." If one inquires about the task of the church, one has asked about its ministry. A final synonym is "action." Ministry is the church in action. That action can be limited as it now is, or it can become evident on a wide front.

Ministry, service, work, self-expression, task, action—all are described in a few sentences by William Temple:

> Among the manifold activities by which the one purpose of God is fulfilled through his church, some attain special importance at particular times and places. To the church in our land today the most urgent call is to renewed evangelism. The heart of this is the same in every age and region—the proclamation of God's redeeming acts and the call to men to answer his love with theirs. But the context in which this is presented varies from age to age and place to place, and in our country today its context should be the sickness of our society and the power of Christ to heal that, no less than the sickness of individual souls. In its approach to the social problem the church should fasten on what is most closely akin to its own message. God created men for fellowship with himself and therein with one another; an earthly society should be as close as possible a realization of that fellowship. Our task is to mold society into such a fellowship and train citizens as members of it. So our aim is defined as the development of persons in community; and we shall test all actual situations and all proposed changes by their tendency to help or to hinder that aim.

The ministry of the church is the proclamation of what God has done for men and his call to answer his love with theirs. The ministry of the church is to heal the sickness in society as well as in individual souls. The ministry of the church is to work for the growth of persons in community, the development of men.

> God needs *men,* not creatures
> Full of noisy, catchy phrases.

You have a share in the ministry of the church. You are a minister, according to God's self-revelation. A man is one who accepts his ministry. Mature manhood means recognizing that one becomes mature in Christ—as a minister of Christ.

There are many ways of describing a minister, or a man, from the Biblical point of view. Subsequent chapters will see him as called, as freed, as sent, as given immeasurable riches. These have to do with the way "you are a minister." Part Two will consider minister and man and how ministry is fulfilled. In other words, this book is about ministry and about mature manhood; the two terms are interchangeable. To fulfill your ministry and to be a man are one and the same thing.

Chapter II

YOU ARE CALLED

YOU ARE CALLED. ALL CHRISTIANS SHARE THE SAME CALLING. As used in the Bible, "call," "called," and "calling" denote God's call to repentance and faith, and to a life of service in the church. The primary connotation of the word is the *purpose* of the One who calls; men are called to be workers together with him in that purpose. The purpose of God, the task of the church, and the whole message of the Bible can be described in terms of calling and the appropriate response. Ministry, mature manhood, begins with calling and is a response to it.

When Paul wrote to a group of churches "to lead a life worthy of the calling to which you have been called" (Eph. 4:1), he was not addressing the office-bearers in the churches but every member, corporately and singly. He goes on to explain why all members of the church share the one calling. Until laymen know that they are called, they cannot begin to grasp the significance of their ministry. An understanding of the statement, "You are called," is therefore essential.

"You are called" means that God has already and explicitly asked you to enter his service. It is as if you had hanging on the wall in your home or in the place where you work a sign reading, "God wants you in his service" with a finger pointing directly at you—and, if you are baptized, hanging alongside it, a copy of your enlistment papers.

The purpose of the whole Biblical revelation is to set forth the call and to outline the appropriate response. Such is the centrality of this call in the Bible that only two choices remain. Either you are called, or the Bible is just one book among the thousands that have been produced in the world, and not what it claims to be: the record of God's self-revelation.

The Bible purports to be the story of God's saving action in history. It begins with stories that tell of God's creation of the world in general and of man in particular. The form of those earliest stories is mythological, but their content is reality. Man rebels against God and suffers the consequences of his action. Then God begins the age-long process which is to result in the calling of "sinners to repentance." God chooses the people of Israel and begins to make clear to them that he wants not only the Jewish nation but all men. Then he sends his Son to make completely clear that God calls them to enter into a new life of fellowship with him and with one another. The Son, Jesus Christ, makes the new life a reality. He dies on the cross, rises again, ascends into heaven, and, with the Father, sends the Holy Spirit into the world to work through those who answer the call.

By the grace of God you are called. The grace of God is not, as popularly supposed, the arbitrary, momentary action of one who suddenly has a bright idea and acts upon it. The grace of God refers to the saving action of God in history. "You are called by the grace of God" means that all of God's action was necessary in order to call you—even if you were the only person on earth.

In the first place, then, God is the One who calls. Your response depends on how deeply you believe this to be true. The traditional wording of the call is "Follow me," and Levi's is a classic case. The whole story takes two verses: "After this [Jesus] went out, and saw a tax collector, named Levi,

sitting at the tax office; and he said to him, 'Follow me.' And
he left everything, and rose and followed him." (Luke 5:27–
28.) As Bonhoeffer points out, many have tried to soften this
story by saying that Levi must have known Jesus, heard him,
and been moved by what he saw and heard. This is to miss
the whole point. The Son of God suddenly confronts Levi,
calls him, and Levi follows. Of course, Levi took a risk. Jesus
Christ may have been an impostor and not the Son of God.
Men today take a risk, too. The whole Biblical record may be
the figment of men's imagination—and weak men at that. What
the Bible says is clear, however. You are called. God himself
has called you.

In the second place, God has called at infinite pain to himself. "You were bought with a price" (I Cor. 6:20) means,
in part, that God has called us by paying a price—the death
of Jesus Christ on a cross. "You were bought with a price"
(I Cor. 7:23), says Paul in successive chapters, to emphasize
the point.

In the third place, God has a purpose in his call. He wants
men for a life of fellowship and service in the world at the
very center of history. God does not call men to escape from
the world, much less to turn their backs on it and pretend it
is not there. The God who reveals himself in and through the
events recorded in the Bible is the Lord of history, infinitely
concerned not only with men and women who are in the
world but also with the whole of life and every area of it.
You are called so that God's love, mercy, justice, and joy may
permeate and change industry, politics, family and community
life, as well as individual men and women.

Finally, the call is God's plan, not man's. The initiative is
his, and the plan is his. Man answers or rejects the call. Nor
is it possible for a man to place conditions on his answer: "I
will come, but . . . ," or "I will come, if . . . " A man whom
Christ called said, "Let me first go and bury my father"—a
seemingly reasonable request, backed by the religious law of
that time. Christ answered, "Leave the dead to bury their own

dead; but as for you, go and proclaim the kingdom of God."
(Luke 9:59, 60.) Nothing, not even current religious practice
and law, is to stand between Christ and those he calls. To
offer reasons for delay, or conditions under which the call will
be accepted, is to reveal the fact that one is unaware of who
has made the call, of what God has done in order to make the
call, or of what urgency there is to the task. In other words,
the call has not been heard. When the call is heard, the only
possible answers are Yes or No.

One reason why laymen find it difficult to recognize the
fact that they are called is that the term has come to be used
almost exclusively of the clergy. Most church members hearing the phrase "called into the ministry" would think immediately of someone going from college or leaving a job in order
to prepare for ordination. This is all the more dangerous because there is a half-truth here. Perhaps it would be more
accurate to say that the primary and a secondary meaning of
the word have been confused.

The basic, primary Biblical use of the term "calling" is an
urgent invitation to enter into a life of service to God, a life
of forgiveness, meaning, purpose, and freedom. It is issued to
all men without distinctions of any kind. A clergyman, no matter how high his office, has received the call in exactly the
same way as everyone else and for exactly the same purpose
—to serve God in all areas of his life.

There is, however, a secondary and derivative use of the
word. Although it is a justifiable use of the word, it is not
Biblical. There is no instance in the Bible where a man is
"called" to be a clergyman or a statesman or a worker. The
Bible is so centered on God's call into his service that it never
uses the word in its secondary sense.

Nevertheless, the word "calling" can be used in respect to
the work of a clergyman—as long as one recognizes that it
can be used in exactly the same sense for a salesman, a lawyer,
a teacher, or an actor. A man leaves a manufacturing concern,
saying that he is answering a call to the ministry. If he means

that after careful thought and prayer he believes God calls him to serve in a different capacity, well and good. But if he implies that God does not call men (using the word in precisely the same way) to serve him in industry, government, teaching, or countless other places as well as in the ordained ministry, he is emphatically wrong! Whether one is an executive, a mechanic, a housewife, the pastor of a church, or the presiding officer of a denomination is a secondary form of calling. Secular occupations (and this includes the work of a clergyman) are to be regarded not as ends in themselves but as means to the service of God. All men are called into the ministry and enter it when they are baptized. Then each has with God's help to discover where he can best serve God.

It is confusing enough to speak exclusively of the clergy as answering a call to the ministry. It is even more confusing to speak of clergy as the ones who "enter the church," for in this case the Biblical meaning of calling and of the church are both destroyed. God calls *all* men into the church and the church consists of all its members. Men are called, not in a general or abstract way, but into the church in order that they may fulfill their ministry, in order that they may grow to maturity, help other people to grow, and extend the opportunity to all men.

Of course, the clergy and laymen have different functions. To assert that all functions are equally important does not belittle the clergy. Indeed, the real stature of the clergy is seen only as one recognizes the full significance of the layman's function. The clergyman is usually an office-bearer, in many ways the chief officer, in the local congregation. It is he who celebrates the Lord's Supper, or Eucharist, where men meet their Lord in a particular way as they journey through life, where the action in which they have engaged is offered to God, and where in a special way they receive the Holy Spirit as Strengthener for what lies ahead. It is the clergyman who is responsible for preaching the Word in the congregation. It is he whose job it is to see that the church becomes a training center where laymen can prepare themselves for their service to God in the world. What could be more degrading for a clergyman than to be blocked from his work by a self-centered and isolated church? What function could be more significant than his when it is properly executed?

Up to this point, the word "you" has been used as though it were addressed to the reader alone. The way in which the word is used in the Bible can be seen by comparing two statements of Paul: "Do you not know that you are God's temple and that God's Spirit dwells in you?" (I Cor. 3:16.) In the same letter he says, "Do you not know that your body is a temple of the Holy Spirit within you, which you have from God?" (I Cor. 6:19.) The first "you" is plural, the second singular.

The first time, Paul is speaking to the church at Corinth corporately. All together—its members functioning as one body—the Christian community is a temple of the Holy Spirit. In the second sentence, Paul is speaking to each member as a person. Nevertheless, it is clear from all that Paul writes that the second only follows from the first. A person's body can be a temple of the Holy Spirit, in the full sense in which Paul means the analogy, only through membership in the larger and greater body, which is the Christian community in Corinth —just as the church in Corinth depends for its fullness on membership in the whole church.

If the Biblical meaning of the word "you" is to be grasped, one has to keep in mind at all times the two ways in which it is used—one primary, the other secondary, yet inseparable. When Jesus says to his disciples, "You are the salt of the earth" (Matt. 5:13), or Paul writes to the Corinthians, "You are a letter from Christ" (II Cor. 3:3), any rugged individualist, the product of Western civilization, would assume that the "you" was singular and addressed to him. He might admit that by himself he could not be the salt of the whole earth nor an all-inclusive letter from Christ, but it would never occur to him that he was in any way dependent on others to be salt or a letter. Yet this is exactly the view of the Bible. In both instances, the "you" is plural and addresses a community. Anyone in Biblical times hearing or reading the words would know instinctively that no one man could be salt, even in his own "private" life. No one person could contribute more than a word to a letter from Christ, and even then would need the help of the church. In each instance, the Christian community is being described, and only secondarily an individual. "You are a minister: therefore fulfill your ministry" is likewise addressed primarily to the community and secondarily to the individual. The Bible is "a message from a community to a community," from the people of God in Biblical times to the church today.

Although the call comes directly to each man, the call is always into the church, to serve God in and through the church, to grow into mature manhood in and through the church, to help the other members to grow, and to extend the opportunity to all men. If you have been baptized, you are a member of the church. You have already been called into the church.

There are many ways of diverting attention from the primary question. One way is to ask another question: "If all men are called, what about those who don't realize it?" This question too has its place. Neither you nor anyone else will be of any help in answering the question until each understands the nature of his call and is grasped by it. *You* are called. That you should be reading this book and not know you are called is beyond belief. The call may seem dim to you, you may be seeking to hear it more distinctly, but you are called.

You are called: respond to whatever you do understand. In other words, don't use a vague general concern for "the people of Central Africa" as an excuse to avoid answering a specific call. Those who are sent to places like Central Africa are currently running into an almost insuperable obstacle. The Africans ask why the people in the ironically named "Christian countries" act the way they do. Why should Africans believe in a call which in their eyes has produced little more than racial prejudice in those who profess to have been called?

God has called all men, and the task he has given his church is to make this known to all men.

When people object to the finality of Baptism, or when they object to its exclusiveness, they have forgotten (or never knew) the nature of the call. They think of it as an option that exists only in their own minds. If the Biblical record is to be believed, they are wrong. God is the One who calls. He has called at infinite pain to himself. He has a purpose in his call. It is his plan, not man's. And his call is into membership through Baptism, which initiates and points ahead to the growth of a person to mature manhood within the community.

The institutional church, as it has proved more than once, can become "a grievous bondage" and "a yoke of slavery." Jesus was promising relief from just such oppression when he said, "My yoke is easy, and my burden is light" (Matt. 11:30). God did not create the church in order to crush his children or keep them immature. The truth is that God often finds more openness and mobility in those who have little or nothing to do with the church. Nevertheless, Christ has revealed not only that he wills to be "in men" but that they should be found "in him" and in his body, the church—in answer to his call and in order that they may serve him as free men.

Chapter III

YOU ARE FREE

YOU ARE FREE. FREEDOM AS A PRESENT REALITY IS CENTRAL TO the Biblical revelation. Maturity, the ministry of the laity, is impossible without freedom. The prophet Isaiah writes,

> The Spirit of the Lord God is upon me,
>   because the Lord has anointed me
> to bring good tidings to the afflicted;
>   he has sent me to bind up the brokenhearted,
> to proclaim liberty to the captives,
>   and the opening of the prison
>   to those who are bound.
>
> (Isa. 61:1.)

In the synagogue in Nazareth, Jesus read this passage and announced, "Today this scripture has been fulfilled in your hearing" (Luke 4:21). Paul echoed Christ's meaning in saying, "For freedom Christ has set us free; stand fast therefore, and do not submit again to a yoke of slavery" (Gal. 5:1).

The fact is that the majority of church members have submitted again to "a yoke of slavery." To put it differently, they have never really heard the good news that Jesus Christ has already set them free. The central message of the letter of Paul is that he was in bondage to the law—the innumerable

42

requirements of the Jewish law. Jesus Christ has set him free!
Until a man has understood what Paul is saying, he has missed·
the basic meaning of the Biblical revelation. "For freedom
Christ has set us free; stand fast therefore, and do not submit
again to a yoke of slavery."

The prevalent view sees Christianity as a set of rules, a
law that prescribes certain "thou shalts" and "thou shalt nots,"
principally the latter. A man will say, "I live by the Golden
Rule," which is a meaningless blob of words until it is spelled
out. Then it becomes an onerous law. Or a man will say, "I
live by the Sermon on the Mount." One wonders whether he
has ever read it. Certainly he does not understand it, for, taken
by itself, the Sermon on the Mount—indeed all the so-called
"teachings of Jesus"—is bad news, not good news.

In the Sermon on the Mount, Jesus says, "You have heard
that it was said to the men of old, 'You shall not kill; and
whoever kills shall be liable to judgment'" (Matt. 5:21). Fair
enough. No one will argue with such a statement and almost
no one is touched by it. What Christ adds is another matter.
He defines a murderer as one who is angry with his brother,
one who insults his brother, or one who calls him a fool. What
man escapes indictment after such an interpretation? Every
man is a murderer!

Again, Jesus refers to the law against adultery. Even today,
a majority would support such a law. But Christ goes beyond
the obvious interpretation to say, "Every one who looks at
a woman lustfully has already committed adultery with her
in his heart" (Matt. 5:28). In our culture, where magazines,
movies, newspapers, and television are aimed at encouraging
lust, what man or woman does not stand condemned? Modern
psychology permits no one to escape—on such an interpretation.

Even though few people know the Sermon on the Mount
or the "teachings of Jesus," they know many pale but burden-
some facsimiles of them. Modern culture is legalistic. Articles,
lectures, and books tell how to be a good parent, a good hus-

band, a loving wife, a success in business; how to find peace of mind, be popular, have the most attractive house on the block. Each account is furnished with rules, rules, rules. Sometimes they appear in the traditional sets of ten; sometimes less, sometimes more. The cumulative effect of all these is staggering, for many carry the full weight of public opinion, modern advertising, and learned professors. If a man works for a firm that publishes "Ten Rules on How to Succeed in Business" in the company journal, he had better get busy—or look elsewhere for a job. What mother can refuse to consult Drs. Spock and Gesell? In her mind's eye these inescapable doctors are like the avenging furies: someday, somewhere, she will have to stand in judgment before them. Whether a man understands the Biblical law or knows it only as it is filtered through innumerable agencies, each of which makes its own additions, the law is an ever-present reality and a crushing one.

Men react in different ways. Some show complete indifference to the Biblical revelation; they couldn't care less. As long as they are allowed—even encouraged—to think of the Christian faith as law, who can blame them? They already have more pressure on them than they can bear. A second group is hostile—sometimes toward what they understand the Christian faith to be, sometimes toward the church for not making the law more explicit and specific. In this group is a man who works with electronic computers. He demands that a group of trained men be provided to feed the necessary data into a machine; then when someone "wants to know what to do as a Christian in any given situation," all he has to do is push a button!

A third reaction is selective rejection. "When I go to work I hang my Christianity in the coatroom," says a man who works in industry. "If I tried to follow the teachings of Jesus in my business," states a man who has a milk route in a big city, "I wouldn't last five minutes." "How can I be a Christian in my work? If I didn't give payola, I couldn't survive," says a salesman for a small business. "I left a business office [this from a secretary] because I couldn't stand the 'office politics' and went to work for a church organization. It was more impossible there than in my first job." "I dislike and distrust my foreman to such an extent that I am ashamed to go to church," says a young worker. All these people have come to the conclusion that the Christian faith is a law that can have no place in their work and have rejected it there.

A fourth reaction is self-righteousness. Everyone knows the man, woman, or child who considers himself perfect. Christ described the Pharisee who "stood and prayed thus with himself, 'God, I thank thee that I am not like other men, extortioners, unjust, adulterers, or even like this tax collector. I fast twice a week, I give tithes of all that I get'" (Luke 18:11–12). The pharisees of the present day, the self-righteous, take the same position. They see themselves as "good" people. They make sure that the law is so construed that in their own eyes they do appear good; they associate only with those in whom they will find confirmation of their goodness.

Now all these people have submitted to "a yoke of slavery." They see Christianity as a set of rules, and they see goodness as a possibility only as it is measured by the rules. Those who are hostile to or partially reject the law cannot long remain in that position; the burden is intolerable. Sooner or later they will learn that they are free, or else they will join the indifferent or the self-righteous. By ignoring the demands of the law, they may, by comparison, find a small degree of freedom, but it can never be fully realized. As for the self-righteous, they are in the worst slavery of all. Christ called them "whitewashed tombs," "blind guides," "a brood of vipers" (Matt., ch. 23).

Nevertheless, even the pharisees are free—if they but knew it. The first step in understanding is to face the truth about oneself. This can be illustrated by the experience of an executive in a manufacturing concern who read J. P. Marquand's book, *Sincerely, Willis Wayde.*

As Willis begins his business career, his father predicts that if he continues as he has started he will become an unqualified "s.o.b." The rest of the book can be summarized by saying that Willis proves how right his father was. He becomes progressively more insensitive, ruthless, selfish, dishonest, and greedy. There can be no question that Willis Wayde is an evil person, for in his blind drive to power he has ridden roughshod over countless people.

The executive was confronted by the book and was appalled. He saw himself the victim of forces that effectively kept him from being the kind of man he wanted to be. He saw himself under judgment as surely as a prisoner who was found guilty and about to be sentenced. He called in his assistant and said: "I have to resign. Like Willis Wayde, I am an s.o.b. If I stay in this job, there is no escape. I will continue to be an s.o.b."

What can one say to such a man? The normal reaction is to assure him that he is not like Willis Wayde. He is a good family man, works for many community projects, goes to church. His work is important to, even essential for, the economy of his locality and the nation. Willis Wayde went in one direction; he is going in quite another. His work may force him into certain practices of which he does not approve, but he tries to remedy the situation; and what can he do anyway against such a vast force as American business?

Although in a sense all this is true about the executive in question, no greater disservice could be done him at that particular moment than to give him reassurance of such a kind. To do so would be to rob him of his moment of truth: for, by his own admission, he is an "s.o.b."—a crude but fairly accurate synonym for what the Bible calls a sinner. What man in business today can help being insensitive, ruthless, selfish, dishonest, and greedy? But before anyone says, "That's exactly what I think of businessmen," let him remember that these same words can be used to describe all men. Clergymen are no exception. The more sensitive a man is, the more profoundly he knows this to be true, no matter what he may appear to be outwardly.

And what is a good father or mother? Is there a parent who has not hurt his child—sometimes unconsciously, sometimes in anger, sometimes in selfishness? What parent is there who can deny he has failed his child many times? Such hurts can never be undone. Over the years they mount up until there is no child who is not seriously handicapped by them. In turn, each child will do the same to his children. There is no better way to destroy a person than to idealize and idolize that person, as American culture has done to "Mom." The Armed Forces records of young men under authority, under fire, or both, often indicate what this practice has cost Mom's children.

The executive who saw himself in Willis Wayde stood on the threshold of a great experience, for the Biblical message can be good news only to those who see themselves—in *every* area of their lives—as completely lost without God. Paul was describing a similar experience when he wrote: "For I know that nothing good dwells within me, that is, in my flesh. I can will what is right, but I cannot do it. For I do not do the good I want, but the evil I do not want is what I do. . . . Wretched man that I am! Who will deliver me from this body of death?" (Rom. 7:18–19, 24.)

Men know in their hearts that the teachings of the law are just. They know that they should be honest, sensitive, warm, and generous, in business as well as elsewhere. They know they should love their children—with the help of Drs. Spock and Gesell and anyone else who makes sense. They know they should be loyal citizens of the community, the nation, and the world. They know they should "go to church," even if they are not sure why. They know that God demands justice, mercy, love of neighbor, a willingness to sacrifice oneself, humility, and much more. At least, many men know this; and under the circumstances in which they live they see it as an impossibility.

The answer that the Bible gives might be stated as follows: Of course, this is what you are. *All* men share with Willis

Wayde his most ugly characteristics. These hurt you, they hurt the people with whom you work, they hurt your family, they hurt those whom you love best. Your record may not be as bad as Willis Wayde's, but it is far from being a good one, and it's getting worse every day as more transgressions are added. True, you are also rolling up good points, both for what you do and for what you intend; nevertheless, the bad points are mounting up. As a just man, you know that someone has to pay the penalty sooner or later. If a law is to stand, violators have to pay the penalty.

That is what Christ has done for man in his death and resurrection. He has taken on himself the just penalty of the transgressions of all men. God does not require that men be good before he will have anything to do with them. All he asks is that men be faithful, that they trust that he has met all the demands of the law—as they cannot do—and that they accept from him what they cannot do for themselves. God has freed men from the law. As Paul said (I Cor. 6:12; 10:23), "All things are lawful" (even though he added, "but not all things are helpful"). For the man who trusts that God has already set him free, all things are lawful.

The legalists are horrified and infuriated by such an answer. The demands of the law must be kept! The legalists of Christ's day felt so strongly about this that they crucified him. They would not have anyone who did not think as they did and, most inexcusable of all, who exposed them for what they were: breakers of the law. They did their best to keep men in slavery; Christ has set all men free.

A man stands, therefore, in industry, business, politics, family, community, or wherever he may be able to face the truth about himself. He is selfish, cruel, dishonest, and a great deal more. He is an adulterer, a murderer, and many other things. No one need balk at such judgments. A mature man knows them to be true, and he also knows that when he turns to God in repentance and trust, he will be forgiven. Indeed, God has already paid the penalty for his transgressions.

A young man lands in prison. His parents begin to realize that their negligence, lack of love, and selfishness have been major factors in putting him there. The situation may have been developing for such a long time that there is little chance that the young man can ever straighten himself out. The legalist has nothing to offer in such a situation except death. Only as the parents begin to understand that they are free, that God has taken upon himself what they know to be a just penalty for their actions, only as they begin to grasp that they are free, can they possibly be of any help to their son.

All this does not mean that the law is no longer of any use. Paul had to remind himself that the law was still vital. For one thing, it convinces men of their transgressions, of how far short they fall of being the men God wants them to be. For another, it points the way when men seek to respond in gratitude for what God has done for them.

In the last analysis, however, all things are lawful. An executive must cut the labor force in his factory in order to make essential cuts in production costs. At the same time, he knows that most of the men will be unemployed for some time if he lets them go. An older man may never get a comparable job. Or a union leader knows that a certain action on which the rank and file insist will hurt the union and is morally questionable. Or the executive who saw himself in Willis Wayde goes on working in industry. Or, to take the most extreme case in recent years, a man has to decide whether or not to use the atomic bomb.

"All things are lawful." A mature man knows himself free to make the decision either way. If there is time, he gives prayer, discussion, study, and thought to the question at hand. If not, he has a backlog on which he can draw. He makes the decision as a free man, knowing God has already taken on himself the pride and selfishness which are a part of every human action. He makes the decision. Then he goes to bed and has a good night's sleep.

Chapter IV

YOU ARE SENT

You ARE SENT. JESUS CHRIST PRAYS TO HIS FATHER JUST BEFORE the crucifixion, "As thou didst send me into the world, so I have sent them into the world" (John 17:18). Here Jesus is speaking of the apostles, the unique witnesses of his death and resurrection. The word "apostle" comes from a Greek word meaning "to send forth." The apostles are the ones who are sent forth as special witnesses to the life, death, and resurrection of Jesus Christ. While the first apostles were still alive, two things happened. First, other apostles appeared who were office-bearers in the church. The New Testament is not precise as to their function and authority. The second thing, which was more basic to the nature of the church, was that the church itself began to be seen as apostolic—that is, sent forth. In other words, the church as a whole and each of its members are sent forth to be messengers of the good news. Consequently, the words of Christ, "so I have sent them into the world," apply to all members of the church. All are messengers and heralds. You are sent.

The natural movement of the church is out—into and through the world. By the terrible intensity of its "in" emphasis, the church has all but obscured a vital part of its nature. The slogan of one denomination, "Send them out two by two, to bring them in one by one," could serve as a slogan for the whole church. Unless there is a radical change, it could also serve as an epitaph, for it betrays a static concept of the church. The building at the corner of X and Y streets is seen as the church, and the task, one of getting people to "go to church." There is a partial truth here, of course, but it is not the basic or Biblical truth.

The prophet Ezekiel has a quite different vision of the church. (Ezek. 47:1–12.) He sees water flowing from below the threshold of the Temple, out the gates of the Temple, into the world. As the stream moves into the world, it grows deeper: ankle-deep, knee-deep, waist-deep. Finally, it is a mighty river. Wherever the water flows, it brings new life. Stagnant waters become fresh, fish thrive, every living creature abounds. On its banks grow "all kinds of trees for food. Their leaves will not wither nor their fruit fail, but they will bear fresh fruit every month, because the water for them flows from the sanctuary. Their fruit will be for food, and their leaves for healing." Ezekiel sees the church moving into the world, bringing new life and healing wherever it touches. The self-expression of the church deepens and grows more powerful as it moves away from the sanctuary.

Would it be unfair to say that the church's vision of itself today is almost the exact opposite of Ezekiel's? The flow starts far out in the world, gaining depth and strength as it nears the church, disappearing in a mighty flood through the doors. The "in" movement has nullified the "out."

The prophet Isaiah's vision is one of the nations' flowing to the house of the Lord. Nevertheless, they come in order that God "may teach us his ways" and that they "may walk in his paths" (Isa. 2:2, 3). The prophetic tradition is concerned with *the world*, with men obeying God in the world. Amos speaks for them all. After blasting the church for its preoccupation with feasts, solemn assemblies, sacrifices, songs and music, he concludes, "But let justice roll down like waters, and righteousness like an ever-flowing stream" (Amos 5:24). Jesus was directly in the prophetic tradition. Although he observed the Sabbath and preached in the synagogues until he was barred from them, his ministry was in the world and to the world. "For God sent the Son into the world, not to condemn the world, but that the world might be saved through him." (John 3:17.) "God was in Christ reconciling the world to himself." (II Cor. 5:19.)

Among modern men, the Christian faith is viewed as "spiritual," divorced from the world, having but a tenuous relationship with everyday life. What a contrast the Bible provides! The eleventh chapter of The Letter to the Hebrews begins, "Now faith is the assurance of things hoped for, the conviction of things not seen"—a definition which, at first glance, seems to corroborate the "spiritual" point of view. The rest of the chapter precludes any such interpretation. "By faith Abraham obeyed when he was called to go out to a place which he was to receive as an inheritance; and he went out, not knowing where he was to go." Few in the present day can fully appreciate the ruggedness of Abraham's task. He started on a journey through uncharted territory with his wife, his nephew, his nephew's bullheaded wife, servants, cattle, tents, and various equipment. The closest that a modern city dweller might come to such an experience would be to start from Quebec on foot with a troop of Boy Scouts, headed for Hudson Bay. Many, sound in mind and body, would quickly choose as an alternative the experience of a man cited later in the chapter: he was sawn in two—still not a "spiritual" experience but preferable to Abraham's.

The author of Hebrews does not give one or two instances of what he means and leave the rest to the reader's imagination. He tells of Sarah, who conceived "when she was past the age"; of Isaac, Jacob, and Joseph, who faced the future with hope and courage even on their deathbeds; of Moses, who returned to Egypt, where there was a price on his head; of so many others that "time would fail me to tell" of them all. There is not a "spiritual" experience in the lot, except for a dubious reference to Enoch. All these men and women were sent into the world, where they had to bring all of themselves to bear on their task.

The characteristic movement of the church and its members is into the world. There it has been sent. There is its mission. Just as "The church *is* ministry" is a much-needed emphasis, so Hendrik Kraemer's statement, "The church *is* mission," is important as a balance to a static view of the church. It does not first exist, and then decide where it will go; its very existence is in the going, for it has been sent by its Lord. For the same reason, it does not wait until it grows strong before it moves out; its only growth is in the going.

No Biblical figure describing the life of man is more important than the journey, man traveling through the world, a pilgrim and sojourner. A man is already on the road at the moment of birth. His parents, his ancestors, mankind—and, above all, God—have already started him on the way; and for that very reason he will, from the beginning, share the way with many others. Also, he will have to travel a route that is peculiar to himself. Any moment of a person's life can be described in terms of a journey. In particular is this true of a man who has been baptized, for his life has been given special purpose, direction, and meaning.

You are sent. If you have been baptized, not only are you, like other men, on a journey, but also you are sent. No man needs to ask where; if he will open his eyes, he will see. He has a family. Everyone is one or more of husband, wife, father, mother, son, daughter, brother, sister, grandfather, grandmother, aunt, uncle, or some other relative. Each has been sent to that family, to travel with that family, to share in and contribute to the growth of all its members.

But the family is not the only, nor the only important, place to which each person is sent. Each has his work. Student, housewife, truck driver, manager, politician, or whatever— each has a task to do and other people with whom the work is done. Each person is a neighbor and is sent to his neighbors even though he can always "pass by on the other side." Each person is a citizen of local community, state, and nation. He is also a citizen of the world. Each person who is baptized is a member of the church, and, if he takes his membership seriously, of some local unit of the church. To this he is sent. Finally, most people have special friends, belong to particular organizations, and have accepted various additional tasks. Therefore, do not ask where you are sent. You are there already.

There is *choice* in all this. Although Abraham and Moses were sent, they were free to decline—with consequences following such a decision. Parents can leave their families. Some do, figuratively as well as literally. Such is the complexity of society that one can easily ignore one's neighbors, the neighbors who live next door as well as those far removed. The greatest danger today is that men will choose to ignore their public responsibilities and concentrate on the private part of their lives. People tend to view all of life as a private affair, which means ignoring the large part that obviously is not private—and the public effects of even the most private part. Although a man can refuse to take his citizenship seriously, he cannot avoid his political responsibilities any more than he can avoid being a father by "disowning" his son. He was born into citizenship and can never change the fact, even by transferring it to another country.

A man who has been called, freed, and sent can at any time say No to God. Although a No does not change the fact that as a member of the church he has been sent, he can always refuse to co-operate. If he says Yes, there are certain choices within that Yes. A student deciding on his life's career is exercising one such choice. A man or woman choosing wife or husband, a person considering a change of jobs, a couple picking the neighborhood in which they will live, are likewise choosing within the Yes. God never dictates what the job will be. Nevertheless, he has made clear what he wants done: his saving action to be proclaimed, men to be called to answer his love with theirs, and the sickness in society and individuals to be healed.

Therefore, the "You are sent" impinges strongly on the "Where will I go?" and "What will I do?" A student deciding on his lifework, for instance, has—with God's help—to make up his mind where he can best serve God, considering his opportunities, his background, his past and future training. William Temple once said that the greatest single transgression against God that a young person could make was to choose his lifework (where there was a choice) on purely selfish grounds. The man who, like Willis Wayde, chooses his work, his wife, and his neighborhood because they promise to be paying propositions will have his reward—which may include the money but, most likely, will also include a thankless job, a frustrated wife, and a pretentious neighborhood.

Such choices are few and far between for most men. The ever-present reality is that you have been sent; you are already there.

Luke tells a story about Peter. (Luke 5:1–11.) Before Christ calls him as a disciple, he says to Peter, "Put out into the deep and let down your nets for a catch." The King James Version has, "Launch out into the deep." Countless sermons have been preached on this text picturing Peter, and by inference all men of faith, setting forth on the fathomless, mysterious, dangerous waters of life. Such an interpretation could have occurred only to landlubbers. Numerous other texts can be used for such sermons; here the point is quite different. Peter's immediate reaction is, "Master, we toiled all night and took nothing!" Fishing is no challenge or exciting adventure for Peter. It is his daily work. He has just spent a night at it with no luck at all. He cannot bear to think of going back right away. It is exactly the same as though Christ had met him as he came off the midnight shift, or after a long, hard day at the office, and asked him to return to his work. The amazing thing about Peter in the story is that he quickly pulls himself together and adds, "But at your word I will let down the

nets." Afterward Peter was chosen for a special task. Most
Christians remain at the nets. Considering realistically what
the rest of Peter's life was like, one would be hard put to
decide which was less glamorous—staying with the nets or
going off with Jesus.

This needs to be said, for one of the greatest deterrents to
the Christian life is a feeling that somehow a man needs to
qualify for a halo before he can begin. The saints of the Bible
were a far cry from the idealization of them in movies, books,
and television. One cannot be blamed for assuming that the
late Cecil B. De Mille must have hated all New Testament
characters; how else explain their absolute destruction at his
hands? Who would want to have anything to do with Peter
after he has been pictured as a pompous, sanctimonious, self-
righteous, fat windbag who couldn't walk a mile without
collapsing?

H. H. Walz has demonstrated that if modern novels are to
be attacked for the evil characters they portray, the Bible had
better be included. As soon as Noah found some dry ground,
he planted a vineyard. When the grapes ripened, he made
wine. Objective accomplished, he proceeded to get—and remain—roaring drunk. Abraham ensured his safety in Egypt by
allowing Sarah, his wife, to assume the duties of concubine in
the Pharaoh's household. Jacob cheated his brother of his
birthright. David committed adultery with Bathsheba and then
had her husband killed so that he could have her permanently.
Peter was sometimes cowardly, often stubborn, and always
slow.

There is no need to continue, nor is there any need to feel
backward in joining such a group. The difference between
them and modern fictional characters—and living persons too
—is that they had a profound sense of having been laid hold
of by the living God. They saw themselves as called and sent,
having been given meaning and purpose for their lives. Self-
righteous men have always criticized God for the people with
whom he chooses to associate. They were horrified at his Son

for eating with tax collectors and sinners. The irony was lost on them when Christ declared that he had come to call sinners, not the righteous, and that harlots and tax collectors had believed John the Baptist, while the self-righteous had not.

God cannot use the self-righteous or those who excuse themselves through false modesty. By their own attitude they become deaf to his call, blind to the truth that they have been sent. God can use men who accept his help no matter how bad they may seem to others: men who are open to God's call, honest enough to admit their own grievous error, and able to recognize that God has already prepared work for each man to do.

There is nothing good about simply being in the world. It leads to despair, anxiety, and impotence. It leads to pretending that things are other than they are. The only men who can grow strong in such a world are the ones who have meaning and purpose in their lives. The Biblical record claims that God had a purpose for the world, died for that purpose, and is now working in the world to achieve it. He called the church into being and sent it into the world to be an instrument of his purpose. In his own way, he has made that purpose clear. He calls all men to become partners with him in the task. Through Baptism some have already been committed and sent. If you are a member of the church, you are sent.

Chapter V

YOU ARE RICH!

You are a minister. You are called. You are free. You are
sent. *Already you are rich!* The riches that God pours into
men's hearts are "unsearchable" and "immeasurable." Sometimes the Bible speaks of these riches as lying in the future:
"that in the coming ages [God] might show the immeasurable
riches of his grace in kindness toward us in Christ Jesus" (Eph.
2:7). At other times, it speaks of them as coming to men as
they grow in maturity: "The same Lord is Lord of all and
bestows his riches upon all who call upon him." (Rom.
10:12). Just as importantly, however, the Bible speaks of the
riches that God has already bestowed—especially on those who
have become members of the body of Christ: "Already you
have become rich!" (I Cor. 4:8). You *are* rich.

The "You are . . ." concentrates on what God has already
done. In this respect, as in others, God's goodness is immeasurable and unsearchable. A rare and finely cut diamond has
many facets. As the stone is turned, first one way and then the
other, the various facets reflect the light. The sparkle cannot
in each case be attributed to the surface reflecting the light.
A full explanation can be given only in terms of the whole
gem. In the same way, the whole of the Biblical message can
be described in terms of one facet—of "called," for instance.

58

On the other hand, the richness of the jewel can be realized only when one has some appreciation of all its parts as well as the whole. Attention has already been directed to the facets: "minister," "called," "free," and "sent." Many more could be pointed out. In order to give some indication of the richness of the jewel, four more facets will be briefly described.

You are empowered by the Holy Spirit. L. S. Thornton says: "What the first Christians had in common was not an inspiring experience, but a gift of the Spirit received and permanently shared. Those who were invited to seek entrance into their fellowship on the basis of repentance and baptism in the name of Jesus Christ were promised a share in the gift. 'Ye shall receive the free gift of the Holy Spirit.' After baptism in the name, this reception of the Spirit was the hallmark of a genuine Christian. The author of The Acts is never tired of insisting on this point."

A measure of the gulf between the Biblical point of view and that of some modern religious leaders and their followers is what might be called the "you can have power" school of thought. The process begins with locating the trouble and formulating a plan. The next step is "to get the power," usually by praying. Extreme exponents of the school recommend measured breathing and rhythmical exercises.

The "you can have power" school is much like Tom Sawyer and Huck Finn struggling to help Jim escape from prison. Jim had already been set free. All Tom had to do was to announce the news, open the door, and allow Jim to walk out. If the Biblical record is accurate, God not only called men to share in his purpose and freed them from the burden of their guilt but also has given them all the power they need at the moment. Mature men pray for courage, direction, openness, and sensitivity—that they may use what God has already given them. More profoundly, prayer is thanksgiving for all God has done for men. Most profoundly, prayer is praise and adoration of the One who has called, freed, sent, and empowered.

Although God has given his Spirit to the church in a particular way, he sustains *all* men. He did not start the universe as one might release a hoop at the top of a hill and stand helpless while it careens to the bottom. God upholds, preserves, and maintains the universe, using methods best described by the sciences. He sends his rain on the just and the unjust, the evil and the good. He finds channels, however limited, through which to work even where men exercise their freedom by rejecting him. Whatever God wants a man to do—it may be anything from changing his way of life to ceasing to infuriate his wife by throwing his wet raincoat on the hall chair—whatever it is, a man already has the power. If this is true of all men, how much more is it true of those who through baptism have received the gift of the Spirit!

You are empowered by the Holy Spirit. *You are loved.* Volumes have been written from every conceivable point of view to demonstrate that man without love is something less than a person; yet the initiative never is with man. John writes, "We love, because . . . [God] first loved us" (I John 4:19). Paul reminds the members of the church in Rome, "God's love has been poured into our hearts" (Rom. 5:5). All men know the love of God in some measure, directly or indirectly, through their fellow men. Without such knowledge they become like caged beasts or take their own lives. Those who accept Jesus Christ as the Son of God can begin to understand the extent of God's love for all men.

There is wonder in this, for man can be described in the most vitriolic terms. If you have trouble along these lines, look up "despicable" and "treacherous" in Mr. Roget's *Thesaurus*. Honest men know that at their worst they deserve such adjectives, and that at their best such words describe what they are like just below the surface. Nevertheless, there is another side to the story. God loves men—even at their worst. God's Son died for them. His Holy Spirit has been poured out on the church in order that all men might know God's love. Man was created for fellowship with God. He was made in God's own image, capable of loving both his fellow human beings and God.

Indeed, loving God and loving one's fellow men are insep-arable. The great danger in writing or talking about God's self-revelation is that one forgets the real purpose of the Biblical record. The experience of the men and women who appear in the Bible is given to mankind in order that they may recognize their own encounters with God, learn to carry on a dialogue with him, and grow in love for him and for each other. Ordinarily, men are able to enter into God's love because they have in some measure known human love—more ac-curately, God loving them through other men. Sometimes they learn of the possibility of human love because they have ex-perienced God's love. Whatever the beginning, growth takes place when there is a continuing encounter and dialogue be-tween God and man, man and man, man and God.

A mature man knows that he is already loved. He knows that God has called him into a fellowship in which he may grow in God's and men's love. He knows that God has created the church as an instrument through which his love, in its fullness, may be poured out on all men and through which all men may come to love one another. You are empowered by the Holy Spirit. You are loved. *You are living under the Lordship of Christ.* There is much evil in the world, but do not despair: Christ reigns! This is no "pie in the sky" or "God's in his heaven—all's right with the world" slogan. The conviction that God rules has carried men and women through the dark-est times in their fight against all kinds of evil.

The world has never seemed more evil than it does today, or the powers of darkness more overwhelming. Small wonder that people are apathetic and see no meaning or purpose in life, beyond their own enjoyment. Unless one is like the man who said, "I read nothing," there can be no argument about the condition of the world. Even such a man might know about the evil in himself and is almost always the first to decry evil in his acquaintances.

The good news of the Christian faith is that Christ has al-ready met and defeated the forces of evil. Christ reigns! His Lordship is not outwardly evident. Evil retains great power.

The final victory will be fully demonstrated when Christ returns in all his power. In the meantime, men are free to choose on what side they will fight. All men are called to recognize Christ as their Lord, to fight against the evil forces in the world, in society, and in each person, and to go forward in the face of social and personal darkness, knowing that Christ reigns.

Obviously, all this is figurative language: no other language can describe the reality of much of God's saving action. A number of writers have drawn a modern analogy from World War II. Like the French from 1940 to 1945, we are living in an occupied territory. The rightful ruler has entered the country, gathered a small group around him, and called for a program of resistance by all who will rally to the cause. The rightful ruler has now left, promising to return in full force to defeat the oppressors. Someone asks why he did not land in force the first time. The answer is that he wanted everyone to have a free choice under circumstances that would test his loyalty. If someone waits until the Allied armies have passed through his village before declaring his undying allegiance to France, his courage is not impressive.

The analogy breaks down, in that the final victory has already been won in Christ's death and demonstrated in his resurrection. And, of course, the language is still figurative just because nothing else is possible. There is, however, nothing figurative in the story's application. A European who had been through the occupation participated with American Christians in a discussion of communism. As the Americans grew more and more heated and more and more apprehensive, the European became more and more puzzled. Finally he burst out, "Don't you know that Christ reigns?" He was not procommunist, or soft on communism, or any of the things of which he was promptly accused. He had fought in the resistance during the war; he knew intimately men and women who were trying to live as Christians behind the Iron Curtain. He simply could not understand how people who had supposedly experienced in their own lives the truth of Christ's Lordship over the whole world could grow anxious, fearful, and fainthearted. It disabled them for the battle against evil and blinded them to the fact that the enemy could not be limited to one ideology or one power but was everywhere.

God calls men into his church and sends them into the world to fight against evil in all its forms. He does not promise safety, much less popularity. Christ said: "Blessed are you when men revile you and persecute you and utter all kinds of evil against you falsely on my account. Rejoice and be glad, for your reward is great in heaven, for so men persecuted the prophets who were before you." (Matt. 5:11–12.) No one has experienced both the persecution and the promise more profoundly than Paul: "For I am sure that neither death, nor life, nor angels, nor principalities, nor things present, nor things to come, nor powers, nor height, nor depth, nor anything else in all creation, will be able to separate us from the love of God in Christ Jesus our Lord" (Rom. 8:38–39). Christ reigns! You are living under the Lordship of Christ.

Numerous other facets of "You are . . . " might be considered, but only one more will be mentioned: *You are given gifts.*

In the twelfth chapter of his first letter to the Corinthians, Paul for the first time develops his teaching on the gifts given to those who have been called into the church for the work of ministry. In the same chapter, in order to make crystal-clear that all baptized persons are included in the ministry and are recipients of gifts, Paul develops, also for the first time, his teaching on the church as the body of Christ. Indeed, whenever Paul speaks in any detail of the church as Christ's body, the teaching is introduced to emphasize that all members are given gifts, or that the church is an instrument for the growth of all members into mature men.

In current practice, Paul's teaching on the church, which he either subordinates or, at most, makes complementary to his teaching on the ministry, is often wrested out of context and distorted. Every member of the church has heard about the body of Christ. How many have heard that they are ministers and that they have already been given gifts for the exercise of that ministry? When a man or a child is made a member of the body of Christ, he is not being elected into an honorary society. He is being grafted into a living organism in which he has a definite function. Just as the eye cannot say to the hand, "I have no need of you," so each minister is to work with other ministers and has a responsibility to the whole ministry, for each is given his gift "for the common good." Paul stretches his analogy to the breaking point in order to emphasize the importance of each member—"the parts of the body which seem to be weaker are indispensable, and those parts of the body which we think less honorable we invest with the greater honor, and our unpresentable parts are treated with greater modesty, which our more presentable parts do not require. But God has so adjusted the body, giving the greater honor to the inferior part, that there may be no discord in the body, but that the members may have the same care for one another." After Paul has tried to make it impossible for anyone to misunderstand him, he returns to the main subject, the gifts of the Spirit.

Nothing is to be gained by inquiring when the gifts are given. Suffice it to say that they are there when God calls them into use, even though development and growth through their exercise may be needed. There are four lists: two in Corinthians, one in Romans, and one in Ephesians. Two of these name gifts; two, the functions for which the gifts are given. Some are not too difficult to understand: such gifts as the utterance of wisdom, the utterance of knowledge, faith, service, teaching, contributing, acts of mercy. Reasonably clear, also, are the functions of pastors, teachers, helpers, and administrators. To limit these gifts and functions, as the church tends to do, to the clergy, is to destroy the ministry of laymen. To require that each clergyman have them all is to destroy the clergy as persons. In both instances, the Biblical record is ignored.

Many laymen have pastoral gifts and should be given every encouragement and opportunity to develop them. A man or woman may be in a position with many people under him. He may be a member of an office staff, a worker in a factory, a parent. Always he is a neighbor. He will have opportunities for patient and sensitive listening, for standing with others in joy and sorrow, for helping in some concrete way, for giving advice in all humility and in answer to real questions. There are some who by the very nature of their work have to act as pastors. Shop stewards, personnel officers, parents, clergy, doctors, lawyers, and corrections officers are some of them. They should be frank to recognize their gifts. If their gifts lie elsewhere, as teachers or administrators, for instance, they should be honest enough to seek the help of those with the pastoral gifts needed in a particular situation.

Other gifts and functions are more difficult to understand: healers, workers of miracles, apostles, and prophets. Two or three, like "speakers in tongues," will require the full wisdom of the church to discover their present meaning and form. Indeed, the full weight of the church has to be brought to bear all along the line, for it is face to face here with a reality that concerns its very existence. There has to be an authority in any body, and each member has to submit to that authority in discerning, developing, and using his gifts, for they were given for the common good and the common task. Until such an authority is developed and until the whole church becomes concerned, the present haphazard arrangement will continue, with men and women using their gifts as best they can and without the source of the gifts being made known. The church cannot be the church except in so far as all its members are seen as having received gifts from the Holy Spirit and are encouraged to use them as housewives, students, doctors, professors, union officials, factory workers, politicians, parents, neighbors, friends. What area of life today does not need wisdom, knowledge, faith, healing, and "the power to do great deeds"? (I Cor. 12:10, Phillips' translation. RSV: "the working of miracles.") You have been given gifts by the Holy

Spirit. With whatever help you can get, discern, develop, and use them, wherever you find yourself.

You are a minister. You are called, freed, sent, empowered by the Holy Spirit, loved, living under the Lordship of Christ, given gifts. What more can a man ask? The pertinent question is how one can respond in gratitude. "As therefore you received Christ Jesus the Lord, so live in him, rooted and built up in him and established in the faith, just as you were taught, abounding in thanksgiving." (Col. 2:6–7.) You have been given great riches from the hand of the living God. You can squander them, bury them, or respond in gratitude.

PART TWO
Fulfill Your Ministry

Chapter VI

A CHRISTIAN STYLE OF LIFE

YOU ARE A MINISTER; THEREFORE FULFILL YOUR MINISTRY; BE A man. "You are" refers to what God has already done in Jesus Christ. "Fulfill" or "be" has to do with man's response. "Therefore" points to and protects the right relationship between the two. Consequently, the word "therefore" is not to be taken lightly.

In the first place, "therefore" is one of the key words of the Bible. It might be called the pivotal word. Paul's letter to the Romans provides the classic example. In the first eleven chapters, Paul tells in detail what God has done for man in Jesus Christ. Then in the twelfth chapter, Paul turns from what God has done, to the response appropriate to those who understand and accept God's revelation of himself in Jesus Christ: "I appeal to you therefore, brethren, by the mercies of God, to present your bodies as a living sacrifice, holy and acceptable to God, which is your spiritual worship. Do not be conformed to this world but be transformed by the renewal of your mind, that you may prove what is the will of God, what is good and acceptable and perfect" (Rom. 12:1–2).

Again and again the Biblical message turns on the word "therefore." "But thanks be to God, who gives us the victory through our Lord Jesus Christ. Therefore, my beloved breth-

ren, be steadfast, immovable, always abounding in the work
of the Lord, knowing that in the Lord your labor is not in
vain." (I Cor. 15:57–58.) The same use of the word can be
found in almost all the books of the New Testament. This is
just as true of the Old Testament. "You have seen what I did
to the Egyptians, and how I bore you on eagles' wings and
brought you to myself. Now therefore, if you will obey my
voice and keep my covenant, you shall be my own possession
among all peoples; for all the earth is mine, and you shall be
to me a kingdom of priests and a holy nation." (Ex. 19:4–6.)
"For I am the Lord your God; consecrate yourselves therefore, and be holy, for I am holy." (Lev. 11:44.)

In each instance, "therefore" is indispensable. With it, each
half of the statement is seen as part of the same reality. Without it, one half becomes an irrelevant statement about God,
whereas the other becomes an impossible and crushing demand upon men. The full meaning of "therefore" cannot be
seen, of course, until Christ has died and risen again. Only
then does the complete record of what God has done for
man become abundantly clear; only then does our humanity
become fully visible in the human form Jesus Christ took
upon himself. "Therefore" links together what in reality is in-
divisible but, in the unreality in which men choose to live, is
always becoming separated.

In the second place, the word "therefore" points up the
motive by which the appropriate response is to be made. As
has been pointed out in Chapter I regarding II Cor. 3:3, Paul
does not tell the Romans that they "ought" to present their
bodies as a living sacrifice. He does not beg them, threaten
them, attempt to manipulate them, or try to force them. Like
Christ, he wants the free choice of free men. First, he en-
deavors to make sure the Romans understand all that God has
done for them; then he appeals to them to respond in gratitude.

In *The Book of Common Prayer*, we find: "Imprint upon
our hearts such a dread of thy judgments, and such a grateful

sense of thy goodness to us, as may make us both afraid and ashamed to offend thee." Man has not reached the stage where he can forget about the fear of God—despite the thoughtlessness of such current references to him as "sugar daddy," "the man upstairs," "the big boss," "livin' doll," or "silent partner." In man's relationship with God, there is no place for sickly sentimentality or presumptuous familiarity. Nevertheless, beginning in the Old Testament and culminating in the New, the response of man to God is overwhelmingly predicated on gratitude, that grateful sense of God's goodness that makes men ashamed to offend him. "Perfect love casts out fear." (I John 4:18.) As man grows in the knowledge and love of God, his response becomes increasingly motivated by gratitude. Nor does God fail to reciprocate. Those who respond to God's call are described as his "fellow workers" and "friends." The word "therefore" points to and protects the reality that "you are" and "be" (or "fulfill") are inseparable and that the "be" can follow the "you are" only in gratitude.

In the third place, "therefore" points to the paradox in man's response to God's action, as we see in Phil. 2:5–13, one of the central passages of the Bible. Paul tells how Christ "emptied himself, taking the form of a servant, being born in the likeness of men. And being found in human form he humbled himself and became obedient unto death, even death on a cross. Therefore God has highly exalted him." Nowhere is Christ's work for man more succinctly stated than in these verses.

Characteristically, Paul proceeds directly to speak of the appropriate response. "*Therefore,* my beloved, as you have always obeyed, so now, not only as in my presence but much more in my absence, work out your own salvation with fear and trembling; for God is at work in you, both to will and to work for his good pleasure." Herein lies the paradox! Each man is to work out his own salvation, as a member of Christ's body and as a person. This is one of the passages where the "you" is plural, and the singular stems from the plural. Cor-

porately and personally, men are to respond to what God has
done.

Nevertheless, even in this response, "God is at work in you,
both to will and to work for his good pleasure." Man has to
work out his own response, yet it is God at work in men that
makes a response possible. There is no logical way of explain-
ing the paradox. One can know its truth only from experience.
In speaking of what men are called to do and of his confidence
that they can do it, Paul adds, "Not that we are sufficient of
ourselves to claim anything as coming from us; our sufficiency
is from God, who has qualified us to be ministers of a new
covenant, not in a written code but in the Spirit; for the
written code kills, but the Spirit gives life" (II Cor. 3:5-6).

God has called you, freed you from the written code, given
you the Spirit. In gratitude, you respond to what God has
done, working out your own response in fear and trembling.
Your every decision is made on your own personal responsibility. Yet God does not abandon you. He is always at work
in you to the extent that you permit him—and, to some extent, whether you permit him or not. The word "therefore" is
made pivotal in the Bible in order that this paradox may never
be lost to sight.

In the fourth place, the word "therefore" stands at the very
center of the meaning of faith. Emil Brunner has defined faith
as obedience in trust. One trusts God, trusts that God has done
what the Bible records, and one obeys—in gratitude, working
out one's response in fear and trembling, for God is at work
within one. The "therefore" of faith includes both the response
of gratitude and the paradox of God's action in man's response. It also includes an alternation between trust and obedience, belief and response. Bonhoeffer wrote, "Only he who believes is obedient, and only he who is obedient believes."

There has to be a beginning, of course. A man may come
to a dim awareness of God and of what God has done in Jesus
Christ. He is moved to trust God, to trust the truth of God's
self-revelation. Then he responds in obedience. Or it may work

the other way. A man may obey, responding to what God has asked of him. If he becomes aware of the freedom which is found through obedience, he is led to trust God. Whichever way the process begins, obedience and trust are inseparable and interactive.

"You are a minister" is an affirmation accepted through trust. "Fulfill your ministry" indicates obedient response. And between these statements stands the "therefore" as a reminder that the two are interactive as well as inseparable. One does not wait until one fully grasps the "you are" before one responds. In "fulfilling," one plumbs the depths of the "you are," of what God has done for men. Nor can one "fulfill" without taking thought for the "you are." There needs always to be an alternation between the two, the alternation of faith, the alternation between trust and obedience, between belief in what God has done and man's response.

But if the word "therefore" is not to be taken lightly, neither can it be allowed to block the importance of response. What is the appropriate response? What is man called to be? In one of the most quoted sentences from one of his letters, Bonhoeffer says, "To be a Christian does not mean to be religious in a particular way, to cultivate some particular form of asceticism (as a sinner, a penitent, or a saint), but to be a man." You are given immeasurable riches—to be a man and to help your neighbor to be a man: that is the ministry you are called and sent to fulfill. In the Bible, the whole Christian life is described in terms of *being a man.* Indeed, for the present at least, the church would gain a great deal by dropping the word "Christian" and substituting the word "man."

"For indeed it is not written that God became an idea, a principle, a program, a universally valid proposition or a law, but that God became man." The emphasis is of course on God. If Jesus Christ is not God, his revelation of what it means to be a man has no finality or completeness. Nevertheless, he appeared as man, not as God, "being born in the likeness of

men," "being found in human form." He came in order that
men might see what it means to be a man, and to free them
to be men.

Jesus Christ does not call men to be God; he offers them
the opportunity to become sons of God, heirs of God, friends
of God, fellow workers with God. Indeed, the first stories in
the Bible attest the catastrophic results that follow any attempt by man to be God or to make idols of his own inven-
tion. All that is evil in the world is attributed to men's continued efforts in this direction. John puts it as bluntly as
possible: "The Word became flesh and dwelt among us"
(John 1:14). It is true that "we have beheld his glory," but
certainly not in the sense that men have seen God in all his
power and majesty. What man has seen is the infinite love of
God revealing what it means to be a man and making it
possible for men to be men.

Jesus Christ was found in human form. Men are called to
be conformed to his image. Paul speaks of being "conformed
to the image" of Christ (Rom. 8:29); of Christ being "formed
in you" (Gal. 4:19); of being "changed into . . . [Christ's]
likeness" (II Cor. 3:18); of being "found in him" and of
"becoming like him in his death" (Phil. 3:9, 10). What Paul
is saying in these letters is closely parallel to what Christ
himself says: "I am the vine, you are the branches. He who
abides in me and I in him, he it is that bears much fruit"
(John 15:5). The metaphor of a vine carries the same meaning as Paul's constant reference to being "in Christ." Jesus
Christ reveals the true nature of man: he is the true man, and
men are men as they enter fully into his life and he into theirs.

The ministry which you are called to fulfill is conformation
to Jesus Christ, to be a man in the world as he was man in
the world.

Perhaps the most fruitful approach to the calling of a Christian to be conformed to Christ, to be a man, is found in a
book by Jacques Ellul, *The Presence of the Kingdom* (*Pré-
sence au monde moderne,* in the original French).

When we seek to discover effective action for the church, owing to the necessity for its intervention in [entering into] the world, it seems as though its first objective should be the creation of a *style of life* [italics added]. For if we consider the life of Christians in our churches, we see certainly that they make good sons, fathers, husbands, employers, and work-men—"good, like good bread," said Aragon—they have many individual virtues, but they have no style of life, or rather, they have exactly that which has been imposed on them by their sociological conditions: that is to say, by their social class, their nation, their environment, and so on. It is not their spiritual condition which affects their style of life: it is their political or economic condition, and from this point of view, they are an overwhelming demonstration of the truth, tempo-rary and temporal, of Marxism. Now at the present time, many Christians are fully aware that this is an intolerable situation, and that if it is allowed to go on, it will prepare the way for the total collapse of the churches of the West. This problem of the style of life is absolutely central; for it is at this point that the question of the integration of Christianity into the world, or at least of its creative power, will be most fiercely tested.

"Style of life" as a description of ministry has much to rec-ommend it. First, it is absolutely fresh. (Could any one but a Frenchman have thought of the phrase in connection with the Christian faith?) It breaks through all the stereotyped and hackneyed ways of describing the Christian way of life. In-stead of presenting that way as a duty, an obligation, an onerous burden too grievous to be borne, "style of life" seems light, joyous, and desirable—much closer to what Jesus meant by "my yoke is easy, and my burden is light" (Matt. 11:30) than the dismal prescriptions often advanced in his name.

Secondly, "style of life" is an accurate description of the Christian calling, for it has to do with the form and expression of life rather than with substance. The substance of the Chris-tian life is given by God; man's response is seen in the form which he, with God's help, gives to that substance. The key sentence in Paul's letter to the Romans is, "He who through faith is righteous shall live" (Rom 1:17). Man has no right-eousness of his own. Through his obedience in trust, he shares the righteousness of God, and he gives outward form to what he has been given. J. P. de Caussade points out that in the lives of the Biblical figures there was more form than matter. Expression is more important than much substance. Kierke-gaard says: "A simple man, even if he were of all men the most limited—in case his life expresses the little he hath under-stood, he doth speak more potently than the eloquence of all orators. And a woman, although she is entirely mute in gra-cious silence—in case her life expresses what she has heard, her eloquence is more potent than the art of all orators."

Thirdly, "style of life" is Biblical. Although the exact phrase does not appear in the Bible, Paul means much the same thing when he writes to the Philippians, "Only let your manner of life be worthy of the gospel of Christ" (Phil. 1:27). They are to live as citizens of Philippi in such a manner that it will be clear what God has done for them in Jesus Christ. The Bible often speaks of "walking in the way of the Lord" or "in the way of righteousness." Such phrases are close to what Ellul means by Christian style of life.

Finally, and most important for present purposes, "style of life" puts the emphasis on being rather than on doing. Whether a person has style depends much more on what he is than what he does.

Therefore, being a man, fulfilling one's ministry, will be described, in this book, in terms of a Christian style of life—which is taken to be synonymous with conformation to Jesus Christ, with being a man in this day and age. "Style of life" is the reflection of what you are in Christ. "The creation of such a style of life," says Ellul, "is a work which is both col-lective and individual. It is a fact for each Christian, who really tries to express his faith in the concrete forms of his life. It is also the task of Christians as a corporate body, where all these efforts, sometimes differing widely, sometimes even contradictory, are recorded"—and, he might have added, shared.

Ellul refuses to give any positive content to a Christian style on two counts: first, because there is at the moment no reality in this sphere; secondly, because such a description would be too easy a springboard for Christians who might turn it into a new law. He is right, of course, in saying that Christians have no style of life at the present moment. He is right also in saying that insights into the ways of God and man are always being made into law. Nevertheless, Jesus Christ has revealed the form of the Christian life and indicated the kind of expression that is to be expected of men. Or, to put it differently, Jesus Christ indicates the direction men are to move in creating a Christian style of life for the present time. And just because there is such a lack of style in the church today, the risk of saying something concrete has to be taken in order to find a way out of the impasse. Although Paul wrote, "For freedom Christ has set us free; stand fast therefore, and do not submit again to a yoke of slavery" (Gal. 5:1), some people will submit again to a yoke of slavery, no matter what is done or said. They will find their law in Emily Post, Americanism, official church pronouncements, or somewhere else.

In the five succeeding chapters, five elements of Christian style of life are mentioned. They are, taken together, an attempt to describe the form of man as revealed in Jesus Christ. They are applicable to all only in so far as they do reflect Jesus Christ. Although the ingenuity of legalistically minded people is limitless, it is fervently hoped that these five points do not lend themselves to making a new law.

The five elements are intended to show the direction in which the church is to move or, to speak more Biblically, to indicate the form of him to whom men are to conform, in whose life men are to participate. The five elements are not distinct but are interwoven and interdependent in a hundred ways. Together they are an attempt to paint in broad strokes the reality which is Jesus Christ.

Frank Lloyd Wright once returned to visit one of the houses he had designed. He was horrified and enraged at what he found. He protested that it was no longer a Frank Lloyd

Wright house but had become the John Smith house. Despite a penchant for playing God, Mr. Wright had a point. One can imagine that something such as uniformly red, overstuffed Victorian furniture negated everything the architect had done. In Jesus Christ, God has provided the house in which we are to live. God leaves the furnishings to the persons, individually and corporately, who live in the house. Much personal and corporate expression is allowed to those who are called to conform to Jesus Christ—indeed, as will be discussed later, personal expression is expected and encouraged—but that expression is not to distort or negate the form that God has given men in Christ. That form can, of course, be both distorted and negated. If it is, man cannot claim to be conformed to Jesus Christ. A man is one whose expression, whose style, is in keeping with what God has revealed as mature manhood. "For the tree is known by its fruit." (Matt. 12:33.)

Chapter VII

AFFIRMATION

THE FIRST OF THE FIVE ELEMENTS OF CHRISTIAN STYLE TO BE discussed in this book is affirmation of life. You are a minister; therefore affirm life; be life-affirming. This is a mark of the mature man.

Over the past century, many words have lost whatever Christian content they may have had in Western culture. "Life" is a case in point. On the one hand, the word has been flattened and squeezed dry under the weight of innumerable "thou shalts" and "thou shalt nots." On the other hand, the same word has been endlessly fragmented in attempts to give various pieces size and impressiveness out of all proportion to their importance. In other words, the church and the world have conspired to rob life of all meaning.

In its most profound and inclusive sense, life includes all the elements of a Christian style of life: it is basic, even earthy. Its most basic meaning stems from God the Creator; and even though that deepest meaning is finally revealed only in the death and resurrection of Jesus Christ, its source in Creation cannot be ignored without distorting and eventually destroying the whole.

In the true imagery of Genesis, God created the world and "saw that it was good." "God created man in his own image,"

79

that is, he created man capable of responding to God's love and of entering into relationship with God and his fellow man. God gave man dominion over every living thing. God demanded a certain minimal obedience of man.

There is, of course, a great deal more to the Creation stories than those four aspects. But of those four, the church tends to stress two, while ignoring the others; and the world does the same. The church emphasizes that man was made for relationship with God and that man is required to obey. The world emphasizes the goodness of Creation and man's dominion in it. Each, the church and the world, tends to ignore what the other stresses. The results are disastrous. Man cannot enter into a relationship with God and his fellow man except in and through the Creation and in and through the ways in which he exercises his dominion. His obedience can be discharged only in the same way. Conversely, the world ceases to be good and man's dominion becomes self-destruction when God and the obedience he demands are ignored. (Here is seen the reality, symbolized by the forbidden fruit incident in Gen., ch. 3: that men refuse to obey, and they have to bear the consequences of their continuing refusal.)

Affirmation of life means, therefore, to enter fully into God's Creation and into the culture that man with his dominion and God's help has developed. God created man for meeting, for encounter and dialogue, and he created the world as the setting in which meeting can take place. "All real life is meeting," but the meeting cannot take place in a vacuum. Men meet in stations, restaurants, and stadiums; at work, play, and political rallies; through books, plays, and television.

And men meet God in the same way. Much has been made of the men of the Bible who meet God in solitary places. Elijah, for instance, heard the "still small voice" on the top of Mt. Horeb. (I Kings 19:12.) Some interpretations of the Christian life make it appear that the normal place for a man is atop some Mt. Horeb. But in the Bible, for every instance in which someone meets God on a mountaintop, as did Elijah,

Moses, and Jesus, there are a hundred instances (including many in the experience of Elijah, Moses, and Jesus) where men meet and talk with God in the very thick of things.

Elijah was on Mt. Horeb because he had had to flee for his life from the king and queen. And the message he received from the "still small voice" was twofold. First, he was not to think of himself as unexpendable, for, contrary to what he had thought, he was not the only man loyal to God—there were seven thousand; secondly, he was to go back to the world and immerse himself again in the political struggles of his day. Although the Bible does hold that man needs to be with God in solitude, its point of view is indicated by a sentence in Luke: "Now it happened that as . . . [Jesus] was praying alone the disciples were with him; and he asked them . . . " (Luke 9:18).

Affirmation of life means to enter fully into everything God has created, into all that man with God's help has created. This in no way negates the true purpose of men, companionship with God and each other, but it asserts that God is met in the midst of life and that God always talks with men in terms of their life in the world. One does not go to a movie, announcing, "I am going to meet God." That would be unbearably pious and presumptuous. One goes to a top-grade movie because it is a product of God's Creation and, consequently, is to be enjoyed by man. Nevertheless, there is always the possibility that one will meet God in a movie and hear him speak. Evelyn Underhill says: "God is always coming to you in the sacrament of the present moment. Meet and receive him then with gratitude in that sacrament, however unexpected its outward form may be."

The word "enjoyment" can be substituted for "affirmation" as long as one remembers that the current use of "enjoyment" gives the impression that man by himself can achieve joy, be joyous, have a joyful outlook on life. The Bible is quite clear that joy is a gift of God to the obedient. "But the fruit of the Spirit is love, joy, peace, patience, kindness, goodness, faithfulness, gentleness, self-control." (Gal. 5:22–23.) The Biblical point of view is demonstrated in a passage from Charles Williams' book *Greater Trumps:* "When her brother had remarked that she seemed mopey she had been shocked . . . by a sense of her own disloyalty since she believed enjoyment to be a debt which every man owes to his fellows, partly for its own sake, partly lest he at all diminish their own precarious hold on it. She attempted dutifully to enjoy and failed, but while she attempted it the true gift was delivered into her hands." Here is the same paradox mentioned in the last chapter: "Work out your own salvation; . . . for God is at work in you." Joy—and love, peace, patience, kindness, goodness, faithfulness, gentleness, self-control—is a gift of God to those who are obedient.

Therefore affirm life. Assert with your whole being that God has not only created the world but also helped man to create much that is found in culture. It is true that there is a strong element of asceticism, of rigorous self-discipline, in the Christian faith; it will be dealt with in a later chapter. Here, however, the emphasis is on an even stronger element. "I [the Lord God] have come down to deliver them out of the hand of the Egyptians, and to bring them up out of that land to a good and broad land, a land flowing with milk and honey." (Ex. 3:8.) "On this mountain the Lord of hosts will make for all peoples a feast of fat things, a feast of wine on the lees, of fat things full of marrow, of wine on the lees well refined." (Isa. 25:6.) The late Alex Miller wrote that there is in the Hebrew attitude "a lip-smacking, exuberant delight in the ingenious beauty and variety of the created world; in wine and milk, oil and honey. It is a world whose paths drop fatness, where the little hills rejoice on every side."

Jesus Christ did not shy away from this strain in his people's tradition. Despite the rigors, uncertainties, and loneliness of his life, he appears as a man who enjoyed himself thoroughly. He loved life and he loved people—two sides of the same coin. His parables and illustrations are taken from everyday life, obviously by one who was no mere spectator but a participant. He delighted in children without becoming mawk-ish. He ate with publicans and sinners without being self-righteous and hypocritical. He could hardly have walked the length and breadth of Palestine, as he did, without appreciat-ing the beauties of the countryside. He ate and drank with relish. He was not, of course, a glutton and a drunkard—as the "good" people of his day accused him of being. On the other hand, he entered much too joyfully into life for narrow, sanctimonious people to understand or approve. His very prayer in the Garden of Gethsemane is to be explained, in part, by his love of life.

Every area of the common life is for man to enjoy: work, play, family, politics, eating, drinking, art, literature, study, television, nature, movies, marriage, conversation, friendship, radio, newspapers, periodicals, music, sleep, travel, and all the rest. Seldom, if ever, are any of these pure joy. Man has re-belled against God, and his rebelliousness contaminates every-thing he does, even after he has accepted the new life in Jesus Christ. For instance, man has to earn his bread by the sweat of his brow: defending England is not the only job that involves blood, sweat, and tears. The perfect job seems pos-sible only from the deceptive viewpoint of the adjoining pas-ture. Work nevertheless can be enjoyed, and God intends it so. In those instances where work cannot be enjoyable, men have a God-given responsibility to move toward changing the work conditions. A man therefore affirms life and enters into it.

Of all the blocks that keep men from affirming life, the greatest is sheer misunderstanding of what life is. Many people would agree that a well-brewed glass of beer can add to the joy of life. It is quite another matter to claim that beer repre-sents "the *real* joy of good living"—no matter what the quality or the brand name. Yet anyone who watches television or reads papers and magazines is constantly being told, in con-nection with beer drinking, "Man, that's *really* living." Simi-lar images are created for such activities as smoking, driving, and bus riding.

All this would be inconsequential, were it not both a symptom and a cause of the sickness in Western culture, if not in the world, a sickness that denies and destroys real life. If man is man by entering fully into life, the overemphasis in various advertisements leads men to deny life, to be something less than a man. This life-denying tendency arises from two kinds of misunderstanding.

In the first place, there is no recognition of the fact that any good thing carried to an extreme is completely destructive. For example, work-saving devices in the home can be a great boon; they have taken some of the drudgery out of housework, which is all to the good. On the other hand, modern "food preparation centers," which are often as warm and friendly as a glass eye, may be more responsible for lawlessness in the younger generation than all the violence shown on television. For their sterile orderliness stifles life.

Television is another case in point. Recently published statistics estimate that eighty-seven per cent of the homes in the United States (fifty-five million) have sets, and that the average running time for all sets each day is the appalling figure of six hours. Television has something to offer—but *six hours a day!* Certainly a man who is drunk is something less than a man. Cannot the same thing be said of the man who has become an appendage to a television set? If there remains some public opinion against drunkenness, there is little against excessive television viewing. How many hours of entertainment can a man absorb during a week without denying life? How many sports events can he watch without becoming a bum? How much can a woman indulge herself in watching phony drama before she begins to lose touch with reality?

What slice of life one chooses makes little difference: when one part becomes the whole, a man ends by denying life.

In the second place, there is no recognition that man himself is a whole, and that affirmation of life means entering into life with one's whole being. For purposes of clarification, it is helpful to think of man as body, mind, and spirit (his will, his inner dispositions). The Bible uses any one of the three to designate the whole man, and all three together to underline the essential wholeness of a true man. Only as man uses all three can he enter fully into life; if he neglects one, the others will deteriorate. Affirmation of life involves the development of body, mind, and spirit. If a man allows his body to deteriorate through laziness or gluttony, he is denying life. In the same way, a man who neglects his mind or his spirit becomes a slob just as surely as one who neglects his body. A man who guzzles quantities of beer is obviously in the process of destroying his body; his mind and spirit will not be far behind. One who watches television six hours a day annihilates his mind; his body and spirit will not last long, either. A man who works solely to amass more of this world's goods is stultifying his spirit; body and mind will likewise suffocate.

To put the matter in a positive way, man has been given body, mind, and spirit in order that he may enter fully into life, that he may be a man. Even with the best will in the world, however, man encounters difficulties. Modern culture has so much to offer by way of affirmation of life that life can easily lack depth. Mobility, increase in leisure time, a higher standard of living; publishing houses, recording companies, broadcasters; growth in recreational facilities, the demands of urban renewal, the needs of community—all these, and more, present man with almost limitless opportunities for affirming life. How shall a man do justice to them all, or how shall he choose among them? Then to his confusion is added the pressures of the modern "success" cult: at all costs to be the "first," the "most," or the "best."

Fortunately, affirmation depends on being, rather than on doing; on what one is, rather than on what one accomplishes. There are bed-ridden people who affirm life in a wonderful way. Interested in many things, open to new ideas, giving themselves to whoever is with them, they are living proof that limitation of action does not prevent affirmation. There are people who have little of this world's goods and who are radiant with a zest for life, demonstrating that limitation of income need not hinder affirmation. There are men and women whose work demands long hours and yet who are able to enter fully into life. This is not to condone disease, poverty, or overwork, any one of which can crush a person, and often does. (Each man's responsibility when such things are seen in the lives of others is discussed in Chapter IX.) But it is to say that limitations of space, means, and time do not necessarily block someone from affirmation of life.

Someone always raises the question, How can one talk about affirmation of life in a world such as the present one—with the bomb, the population explosion, communism, and all sorts of dire possibilities? But has there ever been a better time to affirm life than the present moment? Was it ever more needed? Is affirmation of life *ever* out of place?

Millard Lampell tells of his experience in dramatizing John Hersey's *The Wall,* the story of the extermination of a half million Jews in the Warsaw Ghetto. After three months of research among the many documents and records that survived, Lampell concluded his research "with an overwhelming sense of ashes and agony. I was drained, shocked, and depressed. I thought, 'There is no way to write this. You cannot show this horror.' "

Then Lampell met some of the survivors and heard from them personally about their experiences. He found he wanted to write not about death but about life, and about the affirmation of life that could be found even in the rubble of the ghetto. "Warsaw was an occasion when the two opposite poles of men's capabilities were shown. Man has the possibility of being the most destructive creature on the face of the earth, and man has the possibility of being the most beautiful creature on the face of the earth."

Not by sheer accident did Hersey, then Lampell, write about the Jews. The Old Testament is the record of God's revelation to man that he wants his people to affirm life. Through long centuries of persecution, the Jews have maintained a

marvelous ability to affirm life under the most impossible conditions. Prosperity, especially the present-day variety, has
helped men, by contrast, to grow soft, taking too much for
granted and accepting wealth as a substitute for affirmation
of life. But the followers of Christ have even more reason than
the Jews to accept God's revelation: in the fullness of that
revelation, they are called specifically to be conformed to One
who took the form of man and who affirmed life.

On the same night in which he was betrayed, Jesus ate a
final meal with his disciples. It wasn't an Irish wake or an
American college reunion, but a solemn religious feast which
had been observed by the Jews for a thousand years. Nevertheless, it was not the hollow, wooden, pompous affair that
is pictured in many pageants, pictures, and movies. The men
ate together, they talked together, they drank wine together.
Finally, Jesus broke bread and blessed wine, in order that
the disciples might never forget that, even in the face of death,
and by using such everyday things as bread and wine, there
was to be at the center of life—and in all its ramifications—
a constant unremitting affirmation of life.

Chapter VIII

AWARENESS

A SECOND ELEMENT IN A CHRISTIAN STYLE OF LIFE IS AWARENESS. You are a minister; therefore be aware. Knowledge, judgment, sensitivity, discernment—all are implied in awareness, and all are to be found in a mature man. Awareness has been chosen because it retains a freshness which knowledge, for instance, has lost and because it seems to point more directly to what the Bible holds as essential to man.

Although the word "aware" appears only five times in the Gospels, in each instance it applies to Christ. It is one of the few words that directly characterize him.

"The Pharisees went out and took counsel against him, how to destroy him. Jesus, aware of this, withdrew from there." (Matt. 12:14–15; cf. chs. 16:8; 22:18; 26:10; Mark 8:17.) A great deal more is implied here than the simple fact that Jesus saw them go out, was told about it, or sensed it. He knew all about the Pharisees, what their position was, what their authority, their aspirations, their fears, their jealousies were. He knew what kind of threat he presented to them, and he was sensitive to the way all men, Pharisees included, reacted under pressure. He understood the political and social situation and what effect they would have on events. He was able to discern, to distinguish between, the good and evil possibilities in the present moment, and over a longer term. He had to judge in what danger he was and, if the danger was immediate, whether he would join the final issue now or later. All this is included in that awareness on the basis of which, in this instance, he "withdrew from there."

Similar analyses could be made of the other occasions in which "aware" is the key word. How often one is struck by Jesus' deft use of insights now identified as elements of psychology, sociology, political science, and anthropology! In addition, he was quick to see, able to listen, sensitive to people and events. He had an alert and inquiring mind and vast common sense. All of these are implied when Matthew and Mark say that Christ was "aware."

And there is a yet more profound meaning in the word "aware," as used in the Bible: namely, awareness and subsequent action are inseparable; the one always results in the other. Today a wide gulf between the two is assumed as a possibility, even a probability. "He knows, but will he do anything about it?"; "Knowing is one thing, doing is another"; "He knew about it, but he didn't do anything"—are typical modern statements. Biblical writers would not even understand these, let alone use them. In the Bible, such is the unity between knowing and doing that in the Old Testament one word is used for both. The Bible uses the word "know" as we do— to perceive, to learn, to understand, to have skill. But it also uses the same word for experience. "Now Adam knew Eve his wife, and she conceived and bore Cain." (Gen. 4:1.) "He judged [defended] the cause of the poor and needy; . . . Is not this to know me? says the Lord." (Jer. 22:16.) "He who says 'I know him [God]' but disobeys his commandments is a liar, and the truth is not in him." (I John 2:4.)

The modern point of view is expressed by the man who said: "Do I know mountain-climbing? I've read some of the best books on the subject, and I spent three weeks in Switzerland." "Oh, you've done some mountain-climbing?" he was asked. "No, but I sat on the porch of our little inn and watched some of the best climbers through a telescope." The man's knowledge is irrelevant and illusory. Of course, his knowledge may result in action sometime later in his life, but with such a man the chances are slim. No one *knows* mountain-climbing until he has gone up on the mountain himself, beginning with easy hiking trails and advancing to more difficult climbs and greater risks, as his knowledge, skill, and strength permit. In the same way, knowledge in the Bible is inseparable from commitment and action. One cannot know God by sitting on a porch and gazing, however steadily, through a telescope. "Know," in current usage, has lost its unity with action. Perhaps "awareness," being comparatively fresh, will retain some of the essential meaning that it has when used of Jesus Christ.

The most profound meaning of "aware," as Matthew and Mark use it, is that Christ looked at all things in the perspective of God's purpose for the world. Jesus never thought just in terms of his disciples, the people of Israel, human nature, politics, or society; he saw people in their relationship to God —and all the potentialities of that relationship. Evelyn Underhill once said to a group of schoolteachers: "What do we mean by this faith, this vision? Don't we mean simply spiritual realism: the seeing of all things in the spiritual light; seeing the whole world and all the men and women in it, all the children and young people who are your special care, only in their relation to God?" One can say that if the form of a true man is found in Jesus Christ, a man's awareness is incomplete, fragmented, and disoriented until he sees the world, all men— and himself—in the light of Christ, in the light of God's all-embracing purpose.

Awareness as revealed in Jesus Christ incorporates a wide knowledge of, sensitivity to, and discernment of men, events, the world, and oneself. It is inseparably linked with action. It indicates a view of everything from the perspective of God's purpose—not only a conviction that "He's got the whole world in his hands," but also some understanding of what he intends it to be. Awareness is a part of being conformed to Christ, an element of a Christian style of life—in short, a characteristic of man and an essential ingredient of ministry.

An immediate problem is presented, however, by the difference between the world of two thousand years ago, or even of one hundred years ago, and the world of today. George Gobel once remarked that he and his wife had come to a good working agreement. She made all the little decisions, while he made the big ones. She decided, for instance, where the children would go to school, where the family would live, and when George would ask for a raise. He made the big decisions: what we were going to do in the Middle East, how we were going to maintain the stability of the dollar, when we would discontinue nuclear testing. In a flash of humor, Mr. Gobel has exposed not only his position in the home—and part of the dilemma of the American male—but also the predicament of man in a world grown incredibly complex and threatening. Mrs. Gobel's decisions are difficult enough, as will be certified by anyone who has tried to decide where to live in the metropolitan sprawl or who has had to cope in any way with the economic system. Mr. Gobel's decisions are so staggering as to seem, on the surface, ridiculous.

Invariably, at this point, someone resurrects his grandmother. One gets a picture of Whistler's mother with a Bible on her knee. Kind, patient, wise, she never reads any other book. The implication is that if Mr. and Mrs. Gobel did the same, they could make their decisions wisely. Living in a vastly simpler age, many women and men were wise without reading much more than the Bible. They were also shrewd, observant, and quick to use the resources available to them. If alive today, they would be able to explain to their grandchildren the inner workings of missiles and the politics of big cities. Although Abraham Lincoln's awareness was founded on the Bible, he would have been a poor President, indeed, had he not supplemented and complemented that basic training with many other kinds of learning.

Exhuming grandmothers is one form of the anti-intellectualism in American culture. Other forms are a constant succession of cocktail parties, television viewing, or busyness in business, community, and church. Constant drinking, watching one Western after another, or immersion in "church work" have something in common. All alike deny life and make awareness impossible. They are, in other words, a rejection of Christ and of manhood. To be sure, learning about the world requires hard work. Finding and taking the necessary time involves risk. Sensitivity to persons is all but impossible in a culture which depersonalizes everyone. Discovering what affirms and what denies life is difficult in a culture in which all values are confused and everything is reduced to "good guys" and "bad guys." Nevertheless, for maturity, the great effort is inescapable and necessary. God gives awareness to those who obediently work for it.

Awareness is not a new law; there is no "oughtness" to it. Awareness is part of the opportunity of being a man. Everyone is free to refuse or deny it. Everyone is free to say that a man is a support for a cocktail glass, an attachment to a television set, a drone in a church building, or something else that precludes awareness. If the Biblical record of God's self-revelation is accurate, man, by majoring in these activities, denies his true nature—what he really is. Nevertheless, he is free to do so. The alternative is not necessarily a correspondence course or a graduate degree. Bultmann describes it, in part, as the "need to seek as wide an orientation as possible in the political options at hand—in open discussion with others and in a spirit of both criticism and readiness to learn."

"Awareness begins with self-knowledge" may be rephrasing an old saw, but it cannot be said too often. In a discussion of the family, one woman, asking for help, admits to considerable resentment of and hostility toward her children and cites some concrete examples. Another mother in the discussion reacts in horror. "I *love* my children," she says, avoiding any encounter with reality. Again, an executive stoutly claims that he and his associates are "good Christians" and do all their business by the Golden Rule. Or a union official, speaking of the union's political activity, says, "We have nothing to sell but our virtue." One wants to say to such people (and one needs to say to oneself), "You are free: therefore be honest." It is only a question of time before such a lack of awareness tumbles one into a very deep pit.

Awareness works out from oneself and from one's personal relationships in ever-widening circles. Therefore, the more diverse one's personal relationships, the better. The man who limits himself to people who are replicas of himself is on the run from himself and the world. The chief reason why Americans know so little about Communism is that all Communists are driven out of the country or underground. It is different in countries like Holland, France, and England—which incidentally are no less devoted to democracy than the United States. In talking with Europeans about Communism, an American cannot help being struck by their firsthand knowledge. In many cases, a man will have a personal relationship with a Communist, with whom he has talked at length. The American is limited to the little he has read. As compared with the European, the American is handicapped in his awareness and, consequently, in his ability to act in the situation. He is thrown back on the "good guy," "bad guy" approach.

In a complex world, no man can know about everything. Most men will have to be satisfied with knowing in some depth about their work, their community, their nation, and one or two other areas of the common life—which may be Africa, education, crime prevention, integration, urban renewal, art, or any one of a hundred others. For the rest, they must rely on persons who are experts in the various fields; and an important part of awareness is learning to judge between those who are worth listening to and those who are not. With few exceptions, magazines are geared to entertain and to sell goods. There is little difference between reading them and watching "entertainment" on television. The same is true of many newspapers. If one turns to books, one wonders whether most reviewers are critics or salesmen. They urge people to read, the way clergy urge people to attend church functions. Only a professional could keep up with such a schedule. There is a further danger that one will read only those things which bulwark the position one already holds. Indeed, awareness of the world depends as much on deciding to whom one will listen or whom one will read, as it does on sensitivity to what is being said.

If to know the world is difficult, to act seems impossible. What can one do about the Middle East, the stability of the dollar, or the battle with Khrushchev? The trouble is that from the day of the Boston Tea Party down through abolition, from votes for women and the unionization of industry to the sit-ins in the South, there has been a tradition that Americans are revolutionists, men of desperate and spectacular action. Although revolution has been driven, psychologically speaking, far underground by pressures of the world, especially the pressures to conformity, Americans still have a guilty feeling that spectacular action is demanded of them.

As a good American, Vincent Sheean had to learn a lesson from the revolutionary, Rayne Prohm. At the end of his *Personal History,* when Rayne Prohm is dead, he finally understands what she has been trying to tell him. In an imaginary conversation, he complains: "But I'm no revolutionary. I can't go about . . . " She interrupts: "You don't have to! All you have to do is talk sense and think sense, if you can. Who ever told you you had to be a revolutionary? Everybody isn't born with an obligation to act. There are some people who can't act, who go to pieces under action, who only think straight when they have plenty of time and no noise. But if you see it straight that's the thing: see what's happening, has happened, will happen—and if you ever manage to do a stroke of work in your life, make it fit in. You'd be worthless in any other way. Did I ever, at any time, tell you that you had to abandon the things you can do (or may be able to do if you try hard enough) and rush out to do things you obviously can't do? Did I?"

Think straight, see it straight, *so that when you act* it will fit in. For everyone acts in one way or another. Acting without clear thinking is laziness. Allowing oneself to be carried along with the crowd is cowardice. Being driven from an ill-prepared position is betrayal of trust. Doing the right thing for the wrong reason is the greatest treason—as Becket learns in T. S. Eliot's *Murder in the Cathedral*. Awareness is thinking straight, seeing it straight, so that as one acts, it will fit in.

More deeply still, awareness, as seen in Jesus Christ, is looking at all things in the perspective of God's purpose for the world—a purpose that can be described as God's calling, sustaining, freeing, sending, and empowering men and women as ministers in the world. Paul wrote, "In thinking be mature." For him the test of maturity in awareness was whether one saw everything in the perspective of God's purpose. There are many ways of seeing the same thing. The most immature of all is to see all things solely in relationship to oneself—a characteristic of all infants, some of whom, as they age, develop an appalling destructiveness. One might picture a kind of observation tower of maturity, of widening perspectives, up which a man climbs, step by step, as he grows—from the perspective of self to that of family; then of social, professional, or economic group; next, of community, nation; and finally, of all mankind. Indeed, if Christ's revelation of what it means to be a man is taken seriously, man does not reach complete maturity until he sees all things in the perspective of God's overarching purpose, and his purpose is that all men be mature, helping each other to reach full maturity, "that we may present every man mature in Christ." (I Cor. 14:20; Col. 1:28.)

But awareness of God and of his will for men cannot be achieved by climbing any tower devised by man. Knowledge in the usual sense is important; no one can be aware in the modern world without a good deal of it. There are, however, peculiar ways to awareness that cannot be neglected by anyone who would know God and be a man. This is not to say that awareness can be compartmentalized. It is simply to say that God has devised certain ways of knowing him and man which, taken with other, more usual channels, lead to a full awareness otherwise unattainable. A wise earthly father who seeks the freedom of his son does not give him detailed directions as to what he shall do each minute of the day. He attempts to establish a close relationship with his son, one in which the son may come to know the father and the father's whole approach to life. An earthly father will, of course, have to maintain order sometimes by rather strong methods, but, unless he wants to be no more than a jailer to his son, he will rely mainly on self-revelation.

To paraphrase the Bible, if you then who are evil know how to act wisely with your children, how much more will your Father "who is in heaven"? God knows that men tend, on the one hand, to rebel against his authority and, on the other, to seek the wrong kind of dependence on him. He has therefore provided special ways in which men may come to know him. One of these is Bible reading, interpretation, and discussion.

The Bible is the Word of God; in it one encounters the living God and hears his voice. The reality of this statement will be recognized only by those who learn to read it carefully and regularly—certainly not by those who use it as a source of proof texts or a book of rules. Despite its reputation, it is not an impossible book. The only way to learn to read it is to begin—and stick with it. Although commentaries are indispensable, they can be greatly overrated. More is to be learned from writers who take the Bible seriously, who speak against the background of their own encounter with God in the Bible, yet who live in the world, interpreting God's Word in terms that others can understand.

The Bible, then, is the record of God's self-revelation—God himself speaking to men today—and is apprehended by reading, interpretation, and discussion with others. A second way to awareness of God is discussion within the fellowship on a wide range of subjects which have to do with life in the world, a third is worship (especially celebration of Holy Communion), and a fourth is prayer. Luke writes of the first members of the church, "They devoted themselves to the apostles' teaching, and the fellowship, to the breaking of bread and the prayers" (Acts 2:42, L. S. Thornton's translation). Bible reading, discussion, worship, and prayer are never simply the means to an end. Each of them and all of them together are ends in themselves, work to be undertaken and accomplished by every man—as Christ demonstrated. A mature man prays that he may never be content with prayer when other action is possible, and that he may never act except as prayer be an integral part of what he does.

Nevertheless, when taken with other helps, some of which have been mentioned above, Bible-reading, discussion, worship, and prayer are means to a closer relationship with God and a deeper awareness of God and man; they are steps on the way to seeing all things in the perspective of God's purpose for history. One who learns in some small measure to read the Bible, discuss, worship, and pray need never ask what is God's will for him and for the present time. He will become sensitive to men and events, learn to make judgments with which all men are confronted, be able to discern the times. He will be a man, conformed to the image of Christ; aware of God, man, and history; ready to accept his responsibilities.

Chapter IX

RESPONSIBILITY

A THIRD ELEMENT OF A CHRISTIAN STYLE OF LIFE IS RESPONSI-
bility. You are a minister; therefore be responsible. You are
called, freed, given gifts, and sent, in order that you may be
responsible to God. A characteristic of mature manhood is
responsibility to God for the world in which one lives.

From the Biblical point of view, all men are responsible to
God. Created by him, they have been placed in the world and
given dominion over it. They are answerable to God for what
transpires there. However, baptized persons are responsible
in a much more profound way. They (or others acting for
them) have entered into a solemn engagement, a covenant,
acknowledging and accepting their responsibility. In baptism,
a man says Yes to the call of Christ. He goes responsibly
where he has been sent. He says, "God is, I am: therefore I
will obey God's will," and he knows that God's will, in Bonhoeffer's words, "is not an idea, still demanding to become
real; it is itself a reality already in the self-revelation of God
in Jesus Christ."

Like the other elements of style, responsibility could easily
include the whole style of life. "Responsibility is a total response of the whole man to the whole of reality." Responsibility
is here a particular aspect of man's total response to what

God has done in Jesus Christ. Coming at what is meant here from a social point of view, John Bennett speaks of "responsibility for justice and freedom and peace, for the world problems which harass humanity, for the institutions and structures of society, for political decisions, for the life of the citizen." Coming at the same thing from a personal point of view, Erich Fromm speaks of "my response to the needs, expressed or unexpressed, of another human being. To be responsible means to be able and ready to respond." Actually, the social and personal are inseparable. In responsibility to God, they are seen as integral parts of a whole. In the world, conflicts may arise between them, as when a political action for the good of many hurts a few (especially someone close to the one taking the action) or when larger issues are sacrificed to help a few. Having weighed all the factors and having tried to see the situation whole, a man has to decide as best he can—with God's help and in freedom.

By the same token, the distinction between public and private responsibility can be overemphasized. There has been an increasing tendency in the modern world to make all life into a private affair, and to neglect the public realm—the common areas of life for which men have a common responsibility. The debate on "national purposes" is basically one on the extent to which men neglect their public responsibilities in favor of private satisfactions. There can be no question that increasingly large areas of life are considered within the private realm. In the steel strike of 1959, it would seem that both management and labor looked on the dispute as one basically between themselves. A large part of the country disagreed and felt that the whole matter was a public responsibility of both parties. On the other hand, varying forces have taken many things out of the private, into the public, realm. Teen-agers now find themselves in court, and even in jail, for offenses that a few years ago would have been left to the family or to the immediate neighborhood to handle. In speaking of responsibility, therefore, "public" and "private" have lost much of their former meaning. A man is responsible to God—and through God to his fellow men—for all areas of life, both social and personal, public and private.

Man is responsible to God, not only because he has been given dominion over all the earth, but also because he shares in the responsibility for all the evil, injustice, and oppression in the world. Long after he had had to flee his native Russia, Nicolas Berdyaev said of his country under Stalin, "It is my sin and a judgment visited on me." No honest man can look on evil anywhere and not acknowledge that in some way he is responsible for it, whether it be Communism in Cuba, chaos in the Congo, racial prejudice at home, rural and urban slums, or evil in any form. When a parent reads in the paper that in a rage a mother has beaten her child to death, he has to face two truths: the same murderous tendency lies within him; and he is in part responsible for the conditions which forced that mother beyond the breaking point.

Responsible action on any other basis becomes intolerable self-righteousness. When church members talk, one sometimes gets the impression that the whole world is caught under the rubble of civilization, while the "Christian" remains free. After eating a good breakfast and brushing his teeth, he may work all day at freeing "the others," but he returns at night to a hot bath and a clean bed. Could any picture be more intolerable to those who realize their predicament? To the extent that there is rubble, Christians are under it like everyone else; moreover, they helped to bring the destruction that made the rubble. Within the limitations of the analogy, the difference between those who know the good news of Jesus Christ and those who do not is that the former have been freed from fear and anxiety; and they know that "final liberation" (Eph. 4:30, The New English Bible) will one day be theirs. In the meantime, they work with those with whom they find themselves, and they share the good news where it can be done without exploitation or force of any kind.

Where the analogy does break down is in the fact that all

of modern civilization is not rubble. There is much that is serviceable, some that is magnificent. God has given men the responsibility of preserving the good and clearing away the debris in every area of life. Men are called and sent for this purpose, as well as for ministering to persons.

There is a widespread conviction that Jesus Christ was uninterested in a man's responsibility in such areas as work and politics. He is thought to have been interested only in individuals, in "souls." This has been called the "fishing-rod approach" —as though people were snatched one by one out of the world and placed in an ecclesiastical marineland where they could be kept, safe and sound, until the Day of Judgment.

Such a view of Christ begins by ignoring the Old Testament—and that always results in misunderstanding the New. After Cain has slain Abel, God asks Cain, "Where is Abel your brother?" Cain answers, "I do not know; am I my brother's keeper?" (Gen. 4:9.) As he obviously is, one of the first stories in the Old Testament makes clear that man is responsible for his brother. The parable of the good Samaritan gives the word "brother," or "neighbor," the widest possible application.

God sends Moses to free the people of Israel, who are being oppressed by the Egyptians. When Moses first speaks to the people of Israel, "they did not listen . . . because of their broken spirit and their cruel bondage" (Ex. 6:9). Perhaps just because the story is central to the Biblical record, two incontestable points are often missed. One is that because of living, working, or political conditions, men sometimes cannot hear God's word—"because of their broken spirit and cruel bondage." The other is that God does not want his children oppressed, and whenever they cannot help themselves, he sends someone or some group to free them. Whether the person or group accepts that responsibility is another matter.

The most direct answer to those who would shun their social and personal responsibility and concentrate on prayer and worship is given by Isaiah, Amos, Hosea, Micah, Jeremiah,

and almost all the prophets. Isaiah, speaking in the name of
the Lord, says:

> Your new moons and your appointed feasts
>   my soul hates;
> they have become a burden to me,
>   I am weary of bearing them.
> When you spread forth your hands,
>   I will hide my eyes from you;
> even though you make many prayers,
>   I will not listen;
>   your hands are full of blood.
> Wash yourselves; make yourselves clean;
>   remove the evil of your doings
>   from before my eyes;
> cease to do evil,
>   learn to do good;
> seek justice,
>   correct oppression;
> defend the fatherless,
>   plead for the widow.
>
>   (Isa. 1:14–17.)

Jesus Christ accepted all this without question. It is true
that he would not be drawn into the political factions of his
day, as many hoped. He refused the role of a military leader
who would free Israel from Rome and establish his own em-
pire. Nevertheless, what he said and what he did make no
sense when they are abstracted from everyday life. "You are
the salt of the earth." (Matt. 5:13.) Salt is of no use when
stored away somewhere. It functions only as it is scattered in
the food—here, into all areas of life. "You are the light of the
world." (Matt. 5:14.) As Bonhoeffer says, "A community of
Jesus which seeks to hide itself has ceased to follow him." A
light is intended to be set in such a way as to give light "to all
in the house." Many other passages could be chosen almost
at random to show that, by what he said, Jesus took for
granted that man was to live a life of responsibility in and for
the world.

Not only did Jesus follow in the tradition of the Old Testament, not only did he teach a life that was to be lived in the world, but he revealed in his own person the response appropriate to a man. The Gospel writers take great pains to demonstrate that in Jesus Christ the power of God had become peculiarly operative in the world. He healed the sick, gave sight to the blind, befriended the poor.

Man knows today that sickness has many causes, among which are bad housing and crowded living conditions. Is man to ignore that insight and refuse to give himself to changing those conditions? Physical blindness, though a grievous affliction, often produces persons of great insight; whereas political, economic, and social blindness is *always* evil and destructive of everything good. Is man to concern himself only with physical blindness and ignore the other? As for poverty, anyone in the United States knows it can afflict the rich as well as the poor. People with great material possessions can lead lives of extreme poverty.

If Jesus had talked in abstractions, if his light had been confined to some small area, he would have been left alone. As it was, his life confronted the political with their blindness, the rich with their poverty, society with its sickness; and so men rose up against him and crucified him. Jesus Christ took human form. He demonstrated that a man is active in the political, economic, and social areas of life in ways given to each man. The story of the temptation tells something of the struggle through which Jesus had to pass in order to discover his ministry. Actually, the problem seems to have been not so much what he had to do, as accepting it. Certainly that was true in the Garden of Gethsemane. Never was Christ's life a moving away from, or out of, this world. Always his way led into the world, until finally he hung at the very center of history. Those who would be conformed to him, those who would have a Christian style of life, those who would be men, travel in the same direction. In other words, a man is not a man until he begins to take "responsibility for justice and freedom and peace, for world problems which harass humanity, for the institutions and structures of society, for political decisions, for the life of a citizen"; until he responds "to the needs, expressed or unexpressed," of other human beings.

Many, arriving at this point, think that responsibility means some great, new, demanding job. They are torn between dreading the sacrifices it may entail and welcoming both the escape it may offer and the glory it seems to promise. In fact, for most Americans, responsibility will mean cutting out some things in order to attend more seriously to those specifically one's own. Activism leads to spreading oneself paper-thin and neglecting areas in which one already has considerable responsibility. There are occasions, of course, when one has to take on new responsibilities, sometimes involving considerable reordering of one's life. Nevertheless, responsibilities are never so new that they provide an escape from all the old dilemmas and conflicts. The main task in accepting responsibility is accepting it in those areas where one already lives.

To begin with, each person is a member of a family—son, daughter, husband, wife, father, mother, brother, sister, uncle, aunt, nephew, niece, grandfather, grandmother (usually, a combination of two or more of these). Each relationship carries its own responsiblity. There is the obvious task of being kind, understanding, fair, and loving, within the present framework; and there is the added task of doing something about the framework itself, for the family has changed, and is changing, to such an extent that family life can never be taken for granted.

The role of the father is a case in point. There was a time when the father was the principal authority in the home and also taught his son most of what the son knew—on a farm, for instance. What father has not swelled with pride as his four-year-old son gives every indication of believing that "Father knows best," only to have his dreams of glory vanish as a bewildering succession of teachers, coaches, and advisers proceed to take over the job? Fathers react exactly as do rats that, having been trained to find their way through a maze to food, suddenly find the way barred. Some get sullen and moody, refusing to make any real effort; others become aggressive, attacking everyone and everything in sight. A few have the ingenuity and pertinacity to adjust to a difficult situation. A mother's dilemma is almost exactly the opposite of the father's. As Gibson Winter has pointed out, in the American family "Mother is 'all'." Her problem can be summarized as "how can a mother avoid being a Mom?" No responsible person can take the family, or his position in it, for granted.

Work is another area in which everyone is, or wants to be, engaged. Responsible persons cannot but be concerned both with preserving the good and mitigating the evils in the area of work. Depersonalization, which characterizes modern life, begins when a child takes his seat in a classroom with forty other children and continues as he goes to a crowded university and takes his job in office, factory, or wherever. This tendency is exemplified by a quotation from a deputy director of personnel in the Air Force: "The missileman will be a student of standard methodology. The highly individualistic personality, capable but unorthodox, loses his special value in this rigid situation. There is a new market for the compatible person, capable of accepting the most uniform behavior pattern." Again, "unemployment" is a depersonalized term for the intensely human tragedy that some men, through no fault of their own, have no work. That one easily speaks of "unemployment figures" indicates the callousness with which modern culture habitually treats a distinctively personal matter.

Inadequate pay for some who do have jobs is another concern for responsible persons today. The Bureau of Labor Statistics (under a Republican administration) has estimated that a family of four, residing in any of sixty-four cities, needs an annual income of almost $6,000 to maintain a reasonable standard of living. One does not need much imagination to picture the plight of a family whose one wage earner receives the legally minimum wage of $1.00 an hour for a forty-hour week, or $2,000 a year—*if* his employment is steady. Actually there are millions of Americans living in families with incomes of less than $2,000 a year.

Nor are the poor the only ones whose predicament needs attention. Within industry, the working conditions of executives are, often, as bad as, or worse than, those of many others. An indication of the problem is that ulcers and heart attacks are laughingly described as "occupational diseases." No civilization as complex as this can wholly banish ulcers and heart attacks; nevertheless, executives, labor leaders, and others need not be summarily abandoned to a milk diet and an early death.

Depersonalization, inadequate income, and executive pressure are constant threats in the present work scene. Responsible men will find ways of deepening personal relations, raising inadequate income, and relieving some of the pressure within the present structures of society; and, at the same time, they will be alert to work toward changing the structures wherever they tend to distort, crush, and destroy persons.

Besides work, there are other areas of responsibility. Everyone is a citizen of township, county, state, and nation; each level of citizenship carries its special responsibilities. Everyone is confronted by the evils of racial prejudice—in his own heart as well as elsewhere. Everyone has neighbors, who in One World are almost limitless. There is no need to continue.

Two points need to be made. First, some of each man's responsibilities are unavoidable. As the sign in President Truman's office read, "The buck stops here." One cannot pass along certain responsibilities except in one's imagination. Secondly, in accepting other responsibilities one needs to be realistic and honest, taking one's share of what needs to be done and learning to say No with finality. Here the question of gifts enters. Each person, with the help of others, has to discern the special gifts he has been given and learn to work along those lines.

There is one final escape route that is always a great temptation. Having been convinced that God has given men great responsibility for the world in which they live, one would like to say to God: "Well, here I am. Your troubles are over. Now, bring in the perfect day." And when God does not respond as expected, one is tempted to become disgusted or infuriated and quit the job. Annoyingly, God not only fails to share the opinion that a new messiah has arrived on the scene but also has his own times and seasons for doing things. Furthermore, it would seem, he wants to give all men the same opportunity to choose sides in the battle—before he ends it forever.

Mr. Danny Murtaugh, the manager of the Pittsburgh Pirates, was asked, during the World Series, why he looked twenty years older than he was. He replied, "Have you ever seen my batting average?" Mr. Murtaugh's lifetime batting average is a respectable .274. Although a plumber had better bat close to 1.000 in his work—or he will be out of a job—he cannot possibly expect to bat at the same clip in family and community life, nor in personal relations on the job. The man who tries to reform the school system, the man who tries to treat other men as persons in a huge, impersonal organization, the President of the United States, a teacher, a father, a mother, and countless others might find Mr. Murtaugh's average an enviable one. A man who works for the cure of drug addicts will be doing well to bat .010.

In a Christian style of life, in conforming to Jesus Christ, in one's responsibility to God, batting averages are not known except to God—and he's not saying. Evidently, God is not too concerned. A man is free to do poorly or to fail completely. God seldom leaves a man without some sign of accomplishment—though he never grants the encouragement that men in their pride and weakness demand. What interests God seems to be intention, readiness, openness, faithfulness, perseverance. In other words, God calls men to obey him in fighting against evil and in conserving the good, and he has revealed to men that he will use whatever they offer him. Trust and obey. You are a minister; therefore be responsible.

Chapter X

SHARING CHRIST'S SUFFERINGS

A FOURTH ELEMENT OF A CHRISTIAN STYLE OF LIFE IS SHARING the sufferings of Christ. You are a minister; therefore be one with Christ in his sufferings. There is no more integral part of "human form" as revealed in Jesus Christ. Indeed, if any of the five elements here considered most readily includes all the others, the fourth is the one. If being conformed to Jesus Christ is what it means to be a man, sharing in his sufferings is the basic test of manhood.

The sufferings of Christ cannot be understood except as a corollary of his taking the form of a servant and the kind of servant he chose to be. Paul wrote to the Philippians: "Though he was in the form of God, [Christ] did not count equality with God a thing to be grasped, but emptied himself, taking the form of a servant, being born in the likeness of men. And being found in human form . . ." (Phil. 2:6–8.) Paul uses "taking the form of a servant," "being born in the likeness of men," and "being found in human form" to mean the same thing. Each is synonymous with Christ's own words, "The Son of man also came not to be served but to serve" (Mark 10:45). Being a man, a minister, or a servant is indistinguishable.

Christ's sufferings are linked with, stem from, and can be seen only in the light of his taking the form of a servant.

Christ never went looking for suffering as though suffering in and of itself was somehow good, or even as though suffering was a means to an end. In Gethsemane, he asked that, if possible, the cup of suffering might be taken away. Whatever suffering he had to bear came to him as a result of the task that God had given him and the way in which God wanted the work done. In being true to his calling, he accepted whatever was indispensable to that calling.

Gore's Commentary translates Phil. 2:7, "taking the form of a servant *by* being born in the likeness of men." [Italics added.] It can also be said that by taking the form of a servant, suffering became inescapable. People had other plans for him. Some wanted him to be a great military leader with whom they could sweep to wealth, power, and glory. Some, abdicating their responsibility and their freedom, wanted him to be such a dazzling personage that they would be compelled to believe. Some wanted him to be a model of an obsequious servant, meeting their material needs without asking questions.

He refused to be any of these. Instead, he was the servant of men, who gave his ultimate allegiance to Another; he obeyed God rather than men. As a result, his freedom was perfectly realized. He was in bondage neither to men nor to the world. He was able to accept his freedom as a man and to be free because he submitted to the will of One whose will is good and acceptable and perfect. As it became clear what kind of servant he was and what freedom his calling gave him, he became an offense to the selfish, the timid, the self-righteous and the ambitious—to all who had submitted again to a yoke of slavery.

As a servant, Christ bore the burden of all men. The root of the word "suffer" is "to bear," with the prefix "under": hence the implication of supporting a burden. The prophet Isaiah wrote of the Suffering Servant: "Surely he has borne our griefs and carried our sorrows. . . . But he was wounded for our transgressions, he was bruised for our iniquities; upon him was the chastisement that made us whole, and with his stripes we are healed." (Isa. 53:4, 5.) Jesus Christ took these words as signifying the kind of servant he was to be. Men recognized this in him while he was still with them. "When he saw the crowds, he had compassion for them, because they were harassed and helpless, like sheep without a shepherd." (Matt. 9:36.) "O faithless and perverse generation, how long am I to be with you? How long am I to bear with you?" (Matt. 17:17.) "And when he drew near and saw the city [Jerusalem] he wept over it." (Luke 19:41.) In love, Christ sought out the sick, the deaf, the blind, the lame, the poor, the harassed, and the helpless. But it was only after he had risen again that his followers saw the full import of what he had done: "He himself bore our sins in his body on the tree" (I Peter 2:24).

As a servant, Christ was in the world in weakness. His was not the weakness of timidity or laziness or spinelessness; his was the weakness of a man who refuses to force, cajole, manipulate or trick men into accepting what he knows belongs to their manhood. He allowed all men their freedom, even as he allowed Peter to deny him and Judas to betray him. His was the weakness of a man who sets himself the highest goals, knowing full well they will not be achieved in his lifetime. But his was not the weakness of a man who refuses to join battle, who avoids all risks, who retires into his own dwindling private realm in order to avoid the cost of great deeds.

His weakness is epitomized by those who mocked him: "If you are the Son of God, come down from the cross. . . . He saved others; he cannot save himself. He is the King of Israel; let him come down now from the cross, and we will believe in him. He trusts in God; let God deliver him now, if he desires him; for he said, 'I am the Son of God.'" (Matt. 27:40, 42–43.) His weakness is epitomized in the hours he hung on the cross and saw his whole life as a failure—even those to whom he had entrusted the continuation of his work had deserted him. Certainly, he lived in the power of God. Certainly, the power of God flashed into sight through him. But he had so emptied himself, so humbled himself, that at all times, and especially at the end, all who recognized the power knew that it was God's and not man's.

As a servant, Jesus Christ accepted the darkness, the loneliness, the isolation of his calling. At the beginning of his ministry, he was alone in the decisions he had to make. He went into the desert for forty days to pray about, and think through, how he was to serve God. When he returned to his home in Nazareth, "they took offense at him. But Jesus said to them, 'A prophet is not without honor except in his own country and in his own house.' And he did not do many mighty works there, because of their unbelief." (Matt. 13:57–58.) When one man sought to follow him, he indicated the precariousness of his existence: "Foxes have holes, and birds of the air have nests; but the Son of man has nowhere to lay his head" (Luke 9:58). At the end, faced with the ordeal of the cross, with rejection, desertion, and betrayal by those he loved, with the terrible loneliness of his death, he asked to be delivered from the bitter cup, but accepted God's No in answer to his prayer. On the cross, he understood the deepest suffering into which a man can enter—the feeling that even God had abandoned him. When the whole world has, or seems to have, turned against one, the temptation is to believe that God has too. "My God, my God, why hast thou forsaken me?" (Mark 15:34.)

As a servant, Christ was the instrument of God's love—not an unresponsive, unthinking electrical conduit, but a highly complex human personality freely giving himself to God's purposes. The witnesses whose testimonies are recorded in the Bible agree that in him God's love is perfectly revealed. He is God's love in human flesh. John's experience with Jesus Christ led him to state, "God is love" (I John 4:8, 16). Through Christ, God's love searches out all men, flows to all men, and is visible to all men.

To understand what Christ suffered, one has to recognize that he loved all men as God loves all men. Too much can be made of Christ's physical sufferings. He was spit upon, lashed, crowned with thorns, mocked, nailed to a cross; but victims of the German Gestapo were treated much more brutally over a much longer period of time. Christ's sufferings lie much more in his love for his torturers than in the physical pain. Something of his ordeal can be grasped by imagining oneself crucified by one's family and closest friends. A brother spits in ones' face, a son applies the lash, mother and father mock, wife and friends drive the nails. The analogy is far from perfect, for guilt and evil passion enter into the actions of all men. In Christ there was none—only in the men who ignored him, deserted him, and tried to destroy him. In these, as in all men, Christ saw the capabilities for mature manhood. He loved them. They crucified him.

Jesus Christ took the form of a servant. He bore the burden of mankind; he was in the world in weakness; he accepted the darkness, the loneliness, the isolation of his calling; he served as the instrument of God's love. God still needs servants—mature men, willing to pay the cost of service to God, willing to be conformed to Jesus Christ. You are a minister; therefore be one with Christ in his sufferings.

There is too much loose talk today, particularly in the church, about leadership, as though maturity were synonymous with being a leader. On the contrary, Christ calls men to be servants. It is obvious that in the world there need to be leaders and men in authority. Countless people accept and seek positions of leadership, often for praiseworthy reasons. What marks a mature man is that, in accepting or seeking leadership, he acts as a servant; for whether a man be a leader or not, he has been sent into the world to be a servant. There can be no argument about this from a Biblical point of view. When the disciples were disputing who among them was the greatest, Jesus said to them, "Whoever would be great among you must be your servant, and whoever would be first among you must be your slave" (Matt. 20:26–27). Just as he used the word "slave" to enforce his point, so at the last supper Christ washed the disciples' feet in order that there could be no mistake about that to which he called them.

Being a servant is not the road to popularity or public ac-
claim. It leads often to misunderstanding and ridicule, sometimes to persecution. God seldom leaves a man without some
satisfaction, some appreciation of his work. God knows that
other men cannot stand without any sign, as Christ did on the
cross; nevertheless, a servant is always required to take rejection. Political service is a good example. Men have their
own ideas of the kind of servant they want their representative to be; and when a man stands for the right as God has
given him to see that right, he will have to undergo great
suffering.

As a servant, a man is called to help bear the burdens of
men, to support them in sorrow, sickness, trouble, need, or any
other adversity. Men are called to bear the burdens of others,
not only when the burden is handed down from other genera-
tions but when men have brought it directly on themselves
through their own guilt. There is no need for a man to seek
out burdens to carry; as a member of a family, as one who
works, as one who lives in a community, as one who knows
what is happening in the nation and the world, he will have so
many burdens thrust at him that he will have continually to
grow in strength. By himself, with others, and always with the
help of God, a man carries the burdens of his fellow men by
doing different things at different times: by listening, by hold-
ing his tongue, by speaking the truth in love, by concrete as-
sistance, by speaking of God, his love, and his forgiveness. And
whether a man can help another directly or not, he will always
hold the other in his prayers. There is no more concrete way to
bear the burdens of others.

As a servant, a man stands in the world in weakness. Just as
there is loose talk about leadership, there is loose talk about
power. Power is real enough in the world; but the mature man,
by acknowledging his own weakness to himself and by not
hiding it from others, points to the source of all power for
good: God. Paul learned this lesson in a painful way. He had
a chronic illness, to which he referred as his "thorn in the
flesh." Three times he asked God to remove it from him, but

each time the answer was No, for God wanted him to remember that "My grace is sufficient for you, for my power is made perfect in weakness" (II Cor. 12:7–10). The man who presents to the world the image of being adequate in all things is a man who is serving himself, not God; his own purposes, not other men. In addition, he is living a lie.

There are many whom the mature man seeks to serve: the Negro children in the South who bear the main burden of school integration, the couple contemplating divorce, migrant workers, the boss insulated for years from personal criticism, his own children learning to stand on their own. In respect to these and countless others in equal need, he has to stand helplessly, not knowing whether the little he does has counted for anything, woefully inadequate to the task. In many instances, he can only bear the pain and frustration of being unable to do anything. Where action is possible, it is seldom equal to the occasion—never, where standards are high. Only as one's weakness is admitted, can men see the power God has given in order that one may stand in, and not run from, such situations.

As a servant, a man accepts the darkness, the loneliness, and the isolation of his calling. The church has come to use such terms as "the dark night of the soul" only in reference to difficulty in prayer—because the phrases were coined by men and women who gave themselves exclusively to a life of prayer and contemplation: prayer was their life work. But dark nights of the soul are experienced by all men who serve God, no matter what their avocation. All men have moments or long periods when they know darkness, loneliness, and isolation, when their relationship with God seems to have vanished, and they seem abandoned by God as well as by man—an experience like Christ's on the cross. They continue only in the faith that God is with them, loves them, and wants them, despite all signs to the contrary. One man has to face the fact that he is a failure in business. Another is asked to fill a new position that will make endless demands upon him. A father fails his child. A mother faces the truth about herself. One friend has betrayed another. A student has flunked out of college. Such experiences may be indeed dark nights of the soul: a man living in an evil world, faced by a decision that he alone must make or by action that he alone can take, doing the best he can and finding himself in darkness, isolated from God and man.

As a servant, a man is the instrument of God's love, a person who serves as a channel through which God's love searches out all men, flows to all men, and is visible to all men. If anyone would avoid suffering, he had better not love anyone, for love opens one to every kind of suffering.

Here one has to distinguish, as the world does not, between love and self-love. Since one's intimates tend to be duplicates of oneself, one's love for them always tends to be self-love. This is illustrated by the endless procession of self-protective cliques, dividing the world into "us" (who are good and right and worthy of love) and "them" (who are bad, stupid, unclean, poor, rich, Democrats, Republicans—and therefore unworthy of love).

But God loves all men, regardless of what words may be used to describe them. He loves men when they are bad, stupid, or unclean; he loves both the rich and the poor; for some strange reason, he even loves both Democrats and Republicans. He also loves Negroes, Jews, Anglo-Saxons, Italians, Roman Catholics, Protestants, Russians, Khrushchev, Mao Tse-tung. You name the person: God loves him. Men are able to be the instruments of such love only in so far as they know that they are called, freed, sent, made rich, and, above all, loved. God does not ask the impossible of men: in calling them to be the instruments of his love, he has given them all they need to bear the suffering that such love always brings.

A man works in a tool and die shop. He is called to love not only the man whom he finds congenial but also the loud mouth who is the best workman in the shop, the whiner whose marital difficulties remind him of his own shortcomings, the self-righteous preacher who will talk about nothing but "the

Book." Or a man is an executive. He is called to love those with whom he must compete for promotion, his superiors, those who work in his office, all the rank-and-file employees of the company. Or a woman lives at a certain address. She is called to love her neighbors, the store clerks, the children who tease her children, the snobs, the poor housekeepers, the efficient ones. Or a young person goes to school. He is called to love his teachers, the principal, the good athlete, the clumsy, the grind, the student who gets good marks without trying, the janitor. Men are called to love their fellow men: that is, to see in each person the possibilities for maturity that God sees, to help each accept the freedom God has given to all that all may be men, and to work for the conditions that will permit all men to grow as persons in community.

There is, of course, one big difference between Christ in the form of man and other men: Christ was perfect, while men are always in some measure guilty and their suffering, therefore, is partly the result of their own selfishness and pride. This never disqualifies men from sharing in the sufferings of Christ. When they know themselves called and sent, when they choose to be servants of God and men, seeking to bear the burdens of others, acknowledging their own weakness, accepting their dark nights of the soul, serving as instruments of God's love, then God accepts their offering, no matter how guilty they may be. In penitence, a murderer can share in the sufferings of Christ.

Chapter XI

SECRET DISCIPLINE

THE FIFTH ELEMENT OF A CHRISTIAN STYLE OF LIFE IS A SECRET discipline. You are a minister; therefore be secretly disciplined. A mature man is disciplined—secretly.

The word "discipline" has disagreeable connotations for most Americans. There is no need for this. The root word means "to learn," and the derivative from which the word comes directly means "to train" or "to teach." Discipline, therefore, is the procedure by which one learns, by which one is taught, or by which one trains oneself. Graphic evidence of discipline and the lack of it can be seen at a square dance. A young beginner enters into the festivities with vigor and enthusiasm, resembling a man trying to stamp out a brush fire. He misses the calls and snarls up everybody in his set, which is amusing—for a time. However, an old-timer, who may be fifty years the beginner's senior, will still be going strong and thoroughly enjoying himself long after the younger man has collapsed from exhaustion on the side lines. One is a disciplined, the other an undisciplined, dancer.

It is impossible to overemphasize the need for discipline. Without it, no man can realize his potentialities; certainly, none of the other elements of style discussed above is possible. Without discipline, affirmation of life becomes the rigid

117

overemphasis of a fraction of life or the formless indulgence
in one's latest whim. Awareness is reduced to a few fragments
of knowledge understood and appreciated only by a small
group of equally lazy people. Responsibility becomes willful
"do-goodism" and irresponsible activism. The very thought of
suffering causes panic. Without discipline, a man ceases to be
a man; life becomes shattered and chaotic.

This is not the bad news that it appears to be. Jesus said,
"My yoke is easy, and my burden is light." (Matt. 11:30.) Nowhere are those words more applicable than in the matter of
a suitable discipline. Compared to most of what the world has
to offer, here is good news indeed. Christ calls men to maturity.
His life and teaching indicate what is meant by secret discipline.

The first thing that needs to be said is that there was balance
in Christ's discipline. Too often it is made to appear as though
prayer, worship, fasting, and almsgiving were the whole of it.
Although the meaning of the words "prayer" and "worship"
can be expanded to include all life as directed toward and
offered to God, the words are normally limited in meaning to
the time spent in personal prayer and in corporate worship.
It is important to remember that there were other component
parts of Christ's discipline.

"And Jesus increased in wisdom and in stature, and in favor
with God and man" (Luke 2:52), writes Luke, describing the
boyhood and young manhood of Christ. Prayer and worship
do not by themselves produce growth; study, work, and recre-
ation are indispensable. From the beginning of his special
ministry, Christ was informed, observant, sensitive, persever-
ing, concerned for and responsive to people, able to enjoy life.
Physically, he led a more vigorous life than the average person
today would find possible. All this would have been impossible
without a well-balanced discipline.

The Biblical record holds that Jesus Christ was in every way
tempted as a man, yet never succumbed. In this connection,
one is likely to think of his temptation to quit at Gethsemane

and his temptation to doubt God on the cross. Although there is no record of his early years, except for one somewhat doubtful story, we have to assume that his strength, self-control, and trust in God on later occasions were partly the result of earlier discipline. When the disciples were stupid, faithless, or both, he was kind and patient. When the crowds "pressed upon him," making endless and often unreasonable demands, he was understanding and merciful. With immoderate people, he was able to eat and drink with moderation. His relationships with women began a revolution in woman's place in the world. All this was true because he had learned to resist the temptation to self-indulgence in many different ways, to control himself at all times, and to associate with people without thinking of himself.

When the circumstances required it, Christ used drastic measures. In deciding what his special work was to be and how he was to go about it, he spent forty days in the wilderness, fasting. On at least one occasion he spent the whole night in prayer. Affirmation of life is not contradicted by such measures. Quite the opposite! Unless a man is to sink into a morass of self-will and pleasure-seeking, unless he is to avoid outright denial of life, he has to discipline himself sometimes by the most rigorous methods. This is the real reason why the word "discipline" has come to be considered unpleasant.

Unquestionably, in the Bible there is a self-denying, world-denying strain which begins in the Old Testament, continues through John the Baptist, and culminates in The First Letter of John, "Do not love the world or the things in the world" (I John 2:15). John the Baptist is its classic exponent: he lived in the wilderness, "wore a garment of camel's hair, and a leather girdle around his waist," and ate "locusts and wild honey" (Matt. 3:4). In the long history of the Christian church, there have been many to follow the same path, the symbol of which is the hair shirt.

What seem to be contradictory points of view are explained in part by two uses of the word "world." The ascetics, those who concentrate on self-denial and world-denial, use the word to emphasize the evil in the world and the Biblical belief that the world is in the grip of evil forces. While agreeing that the "powers of darkness" still have a firm hold on things and that man in rebelling against God has become unable to cope with evil, the second point of view concentrates on the reality that the world is God's creation. God found it good and sent his Son to die for it. The victory over evil was won on the cross and in the resurrection, to be finally revealed "in the last day." Jesus Christ not only made this point of view possible but also was in this second tradition himself. A modern writer who takes the same position says: "My deepest and most un-shakable conviction is that, whatever all the thinkers and doc-tors have said, it is not God's will at all to be loved by us *against* the Creation, but rather glorified *through* the Creation and with the Creation as our starting point. That is why I find so many devotional books intolerable!"

Nevertheless, asceticism—a self-denying, world-denying dis-cipline—is a part of Christ's life. In fact, it is indispensable to anyone who would achieve self-control and give himself com-pletely to some particular purpose. Every once in a while the sports writers discover a runner who claims that the "secret" of his success is a diet of something like beef juice and raw turnips. There is, of course, no secret to being a good runner: it is simply a matter of native ability, rigorous discipline, and, usually, good coaching. The beef juice and raw turnips are more likely to be symbols of the self-denial and world-denial to which a man will submit in order to attain his goal. Asceti-cism is an integral part of any noble endeavor. It will be found in business, in labor unions, in politics, in the theater, in music, in welfare work, and in a hundred other places.

Nevertheless, asceticism and the other parts of any discipline can be just as easily directed toward evil purposes as toward good ones. A variant of the question, What do you want to be? is, Where are you going? With its corollary, How seriously do you want to get there? the question of direction is basic for discipline. It is at this point that prayer and worship are seen most clearly in the discipline of Jesus Christ. His was a life lived in the deepest possible relationship with God. "He humbled himself and became obedient unto death, even death on a cross" (Phil. 2:8) is the measure of his resolute courage and perseverance. He may be described as a man who never deviated in his direction. Prayer and worship were what kept his destination in sight. "He learned obedience through what he suffered" (Heb. 5:8), that is, through misunderstanding, rejection, weakness, failure, and pain. Countless people have been turned aside through such experiences or have had their commitment to evil purposes deepened. Only through prayer and worship can man be with God in such circumstances: only by seeing all things in the light of Jesus Christ, only by seeking a continuing relationship with God, only in offering all that one does to God.

In prayer and worship, one sees that the question of direction is primary. Such questions as, Is this useful? and Will I be successful? take their proper place. Sometimes they are valid questions, but they are not nearly so important as modern culture insists. In prayer and worship, one learns that God can use all that one does for his purposes: the frustrations, mistakes, failures—even outright rebelliousness—when they are offered to him. Through prayer and worship all life becomes meaningful and purposeful. Man is seen for the greatness that is in him, as sharing in the glory and purpose of God.

Prayer and worship, like other parts of a discipline, do not come naturally to most men any more than do skill at games or ability to study. Indeed, they become tolerable only when seen as directly relevant to life. The trouble with many devotional books is that they deal with the "inner life" as though it existed independently of life in the world. Nothing could be farther from reality as revealed in Jesus Christ. For him, prayer was always intimately connected with the work he had been given to do and the life to which he had been called. He prayed about the decisions he had to make, the people with whom he lived and worked, the problems he had to meet the next day or the next minute. He wept over Jerusalem, he asked God to forgive those who nailed him to the cross, he prayed that God would be with those who were to carry on his work after him. There was such a wholeness to Christ's life that "inner" and "outer" become practically indistinguishable. Whatever a man's work, whatever his relationships, whatever his responsibilities, being conformed to Jesus Christ means that his prayer and worship are an integral part of his whole life.

The balance and integrity of Christ's discipline, the depth and direction that it gave to his life, are shown in his submission to the men who tried, sentenced, and executed him. Although it would be a classic understatement to say that they were "not fit to unfasten his shoes" (Luke 3:16, The New English Bible), he submitted to their authority. A lifetime of discipline is represented here. He would not have hesitated to oppose them in any way that he believed God demanded. In fact, he did just that in telling them the truth about themselves on more than one occasion, opposition that they found intolerable and that took much more discipline than armed rebellion. In the end, however, he went to his death "like a lamb that is led to the slaughter, and like a sheep that before its shearers is dumb" (Isa. 53:7). Is there a more direct test of a man's discipline, of his maturity, than his reaction to authority?

That Jesus Christ was a thoroughly disciplined person is evident to anyone who takes the trouble to search a bit; that he urged secrecy in discipline is immediately apparent. His attitude may be summarized by saying that he took discipline for granted and went out of his way to insist on secrecy. His own discipline was so secret that it had to be deduced from the results, and from casual remarks made by him and by those who wrote about him.

No deductions are needed to arrive at the conclusion that

Christ believed in *secret* discipline. "When you give alms, sound no trumpet before you; . . . do not let your left hand know what your right hand is doing." (Matt. 6:2, 3.) "When you pray, go into your room and shut the door." (Matt. 6:6.) "When you fast, anoint your head and wash your face, that your fasting may not be seen by men." (Matt. 6:17, 18.) In each case, the man who prays, fasts, or gives alms to be seen by men will be seen by men, and that is the only reward he will have. Christ does not contrast the praying, fasting, and almsgiving that is done to be seen by men with the kind done oblivious to whether men see or not, condemning the first and approving the second. He goes much farther to say: make every effort that no one except God will see you. In the case of alms, at least, he goes as far as one can go, by urging his listeners not to let their left hand know what their right hand is doing. In other words, keep your charities a secret—even from yourself. Could anything be clearer than that? Secrecy is not optional or advisable or commendable—it is absolutely essential.

And could anything be more contrary to this than current practice? A hundred methods have been devised for publicizing almsgiving, prayer, fasting, and all parts of discipline. A church group performs an act of charity—and sends a notice to the local newspaper. People are urged to wear insignia, which not only broadcasts the claim that the wearer prays but encourages others to ask questions that lead to further opportunities for publicity. Fasting has become an endless topic of conversation and a source of big business. Athletes, industrialists, politicians, any who are considered sufficiently "successful," are encouraged to "tell all," in detail and with pictures.

Secrecy is indispensable to the existence of personhood and to the growth of persons. Man knows and responds to God and his fellow men in the deepest, most private, most hidden area of his life. When this hiddenness is dissipated, either by his own choice or through pressures from outside, a man is no longer able to enter into meaningful relationships with others. Discipline belongs to the area of personal life that needs to be kept hidden. The cost of indiscriminate revealing of one's discipline is to lose it altogether or to make it into a law. The man who has to tell about his body-building exercises, his methods of self-education, or his prayer life is a man under law, and he wants all men to acknowledge its validity. Silence and solitude are integral to the growth of a mature man, for it is in silence and solitude that a man can best know his own integrity and his oneness with God and with men. Christ's insistence on secrecy can be appreciated by remembering that in the Bible, marriage is regarded as the closest analogy to the relationship between Christ and his church. A mature man will talk about his marriage when he needs help or when it is reasonably clear that others need and can accept his help; otherwise, to talk about one's marriage is to destroy it, or to reveal that it is already destroyed.

Discipline cannot be understood as long as it is viewed solely as a means to an end. If it were just this, the admonition to secrecy would be hard to justify. Discipline is, however, both a means and an end. Adequate exercise can be a grim matter of deep breathing and push-ups—slow death for all but the most literal-minded. But, with a little imagination and ingenuity, it can also be a thanksgiving for creation in general and for one's body in particular—a time of friendship and renewal. Study can be treated as simply a means: one can study as "preparation for life" or as "learning a trade." But study can also be an end as well as a means, pursued for the joy of learning, for the opening of new worlds, for a knowledge of all creation.

Discipline as both end and means can be seen in two disciplines not yet mentioned. The first is Bible study. For those who accept the Bible as the record of God's self-revelation, it provides the best means of learning about God, of knowing his will, and of discovering the context of responsible decision and of real life. But the Bible is much more. It is a place in which God is encountered and a dialogue with him takes place: in other words, Bible study is an end in itself. The same may be said of participation in the Christian fellowship, in discussion as well as in corporate worship, in sharing the common life. It is a means to knowing God; but it also provides moments in which encounter and dialogue with God and men take place, and it needs, therefore, no further justification.

Christ leaves each man free to develop his own discipline. There is no area in which man is more on his own to work out his own salvation. Each man has, with the help of God and the fellowship, to consider his call, to recognize where and to whom he has been sent, to think of his own affirmation or denial of life, and to decide what steps are necessary and possible for him. Does he have to discipline himself, even at considerable cost to himself, in the time he gives to work? Does he give adequate time and energy to politics and other public responsibilities? How much time can he give to television, magazines, the daily newspaper? If on the one hand he relinquishes the image of himself at twenty, and on the other hand remembers the drain of a flabby body on mind and spirit, what does he need in the way of exercise? To what degree can he indulge himself in eating, drinking, or following the whim of the moment? Does he appreciate the need for Bible study, discussion within the fellowship, worship, and prayer?

These are some of the questions that a mature man asks himself. He approaches them, however, as a free person. God will not become disgusted with him, let alone reject him, when he fails again and again. Nor is he required to make out a complete time schedule for every day in the week, expecting of himself what he demands of the local railroad or bus company.

In considering discipline, especially in the attempt to achieve balance, there is always danger that it will become burden and law. That is why the discipline of a mature man is secret.

In the most private, deepest, most hidden area of a man's life, he can know most intensely the freedom he has been given by God. Here he can work out his own discipline in fear and trembling, assured that God is ready to help, is already at work in him. Here a man does what he as a person feels called to do, that he may thankfully direct and order his life in accordance with God's will. Here he accepts the disciplines that will bring him into ever closer relationship with God and that, in themselves, provide a time and a place of encounter and dialogue with God and man.

CONCLUSION

You ARE A MINISTER OF CHRIST; THEREFORE FULFILL YOUR ministry, be a man, a servant of the living Christ in the world. If you are baptized, you are a minister whether you are ordained or not. All men are called into the church by God for a life of service in the world. All men have been freed by the death of Christ on the cross. Through Christ, immeasurable riches have been made available to all men. As a baptized person, you have said Yes to the call, you have accepted your freedom and the other gifts of God, and you have been sent into the world.

Therefore be a mature man: affirm life, be aware, be responsible, be one with Christ in his suffering, be secretly disciplined. God has acted in history in order that all men may reach maturity. Only in their maturity can God have the relationship with men that he seeks with all. Only to the extent that men are mature can they be his instrument in the healing of the sickness in society and in individual souls. Jesus Christ took the form of man that men might know what manhood was and, in being conformed to him, might reach maturity.

In the church today, many a discussion shows general agreement with much of what has here been said about the ministry of the laity. Almost invariably such discussions end on an optimistic note. "Great things are happening!" "Many thrilling experiments are being undertaken in various parts of the church!" "We are finally moving toward a real ministry of the laity!" The conversation ends on this optimistic note, and any further encounter with the realities of the situation is effectively postponed. In face of such an optimistic outlook, three things need to be said.

In the first place, there is a half-truth here. Some people do see the need for a ministry of the laity that takes the life and work of men and women in the world as seriously as the life and work of the clergy within the institutional church. They are moving, often at great risk and cost, to find ways of making the ministry of the laity a reality. Some have gone to such lengths that local congregations have split in two: on the one side, those who feel that the church has to engage the world; on the other, those who want the church to remain solely a place of comfort.

But those who see the need and try to move toward meeting it are not optimistic. They could not continue, of course, did they not trust that God accepts their obedience, however imperfect, and uses their efforts for his purpose, which, they believe, will eventually mean a renewal of the church. Nevertheless, they know that concrete evidence of achievement is sparse.

In the second place, for every man and woman who takes the ministry of the laity seriously, there are at least ten who pay it no more than lip service—and forty who couldn't care less. It cannot be said too often that, for all the talk of a brave new world, the layman remains a second-class citizen, in bondage to an overinstitutionalized church. How many laymen, in the last ten years, have begun to see that their ministry lies in the world and have turned hopefully to their church for help, only to have been sold into slavery for maintenance work or housekeeping duties in an omnivorous institution?

In case someone thinks this an overstatement, consider a church that decided to "find a place for laymen in its ministry."

Each member of the governing board was made chairman of a commission, each commission had five to eight committees, each committee had subcommittees. The net result? More than 50 per cent of the members of the congregation were active in some group, and *not one of the groups* had anything to do with everyday work, local or national politics, international affairs, a realistic attempt to come to grips with family life, or anything else that was of vital interest to laymen living and working in the world. Although there was a liturgical commission and a committee or subcommittee on prayer, they seemed to have little more relevance to life in the world than did the properties commission and the kitchen committee. The only exceptional thing about this church was the ingenuity and thoroughness with which it was organized. How can one remain optimistic when such a church continues to be held up as a model for others to copy?

Laymen either escape from such a situation to the freer air of the world or become "clericalized laymen" or good-naturedly adjust themselves—and never achieve the maturity of which they are capable. That some organization is necessary, that some congregations, even with commissions, committees, and subcommittees, try to engage the world, does not excuse the horror, the destructiveness, the irrelevance of the over-organized, self-centered church.

In the third place, "optimists" are usually "gradualists." They maintain that the church has the time to change slowly, avoiding the controversy, the risk, and the cost of renewal *now*. They believe that churches and denominations have the stability and enough strength to continue as they are, while change is gradually introduced. They may be right. Then again, they may be as deluded as the gradualists in racial integration, who thought there was time for gradual change when there was not. (Already it may be too late for peaceful, constructive change in that area; at any rate, there is now very little time to do what cried out to be done many years ago.) The development of a ministry of the laity is as urgent and imperative for the church as a solution of the racial problem is for the United States. There may be even less time for the church. The "gates of hell shall not prevail" against the church; but churches and denominations—be they Protestant, Catholic, or Orthodox—have been, and can again be, destroyed. As even a cursory reading of the Bible will indicate, the wrath of God "poured out" on the disobedient is nothing to look forward to, or minimize.

To return to Ezekiel's vision of the river flowing from the altar into the world, those concerned with the ministry of the laity know that the river is flowing from the world to disappear into church buildings. Only when the river is reversed and the normal movement of the church is into the world will there be a genuine ministry of the laity.

In other words, the whole direction of the church has to be reversed. At the moment, it is turned in on itself, obsessed with its own self-preservation, concentrating on "growth without evolution." In addition, the life of the church is constricted by forms inherited from the nineteenth century and earlier. The world has changed more in the past one hundred and fifty years than in the previous eighteen hundred, while the church has remained practically the same. All this has been said over and over again by many people. The church does not hear. Anyone who loves it cannot but tremble at the "shaking of the foundations" that lies ahead.

"Community" is a case in point. Sociologists, psychologists, anthropologists, and theologians agree that the breakdown of community is one of the scourges of modern civilization. Those who suffer both from the breakdown of community and from the analysis of the experts agree. The church has recognized the need and tried to help—on the whole, ineffectually. In its isolation, it has tried to encourage prayer and study groups, to deepen worship—in the familiar term, to create fellowship. Little has been accomplished because community is impossible without economic, political, familial, and social— as well as spiritual—foundations. Indeed, in community of any depth, it is difficult to differentiate one factor from another.

Two hundred years ago, the larger, deeper, broader community could be taken for granted. There was coherence and unity to an extent unknown today. Within that community and truly representative of it, the church could meet for worship which gathered up, and was reflected in, all areas of the common life. Today, the church is challenged by the task of helping to create community in all its aspects. Bonhoeffer once wrote, "I often ask myself why a Christian instinct frequently draws me more to the religionless than to the religious, by which I mean not with any intention of evangelizing them, but rather, I might almost say, in 'brotherhood.'" The answer may lie in William Temple's much-quoted statement, "God is not primarily interested in religion." Men can meet God and one another on a deeper level when they are in politics together or when they work together, than when they meet to be religious. They will meet on the deepest level when prayer and politics, worship and work, Bible study and neighborliness, are interwoven in countless ways. In the meantime, religious practices have little value in a vacuum, and the breakdown of community continues.

To put the matter differently, unless a man takes politics seriously, he is not mature; he is not being conformed to Jesus Christ in the full meaning of Paul's phrase. It is no mere coincidence that as a nation Americans grow soft at a time when affluence leads men to concentrate on their own comfort and security. Nor is it coincidence that men mature as they strive together against the evil forces in the world and in themselves. Although the musical purists may scoff at it, "Stand Up, Stand Up for Jesus" remains, for many people, one of the most stirring of hymns. With good reason! It was written by a man for his friend who lay dying. Together, in the name of God, they had fought against racial prejudice and many kinds of injustice. The hymn expresses their strong faith and deep fellowship. "Community," says Ronald Gregor Smith, "is the being together in responsible action." Imagine, if you can, a man writing a hymn for another with whom he had shared the task of ushering on Sunday morning. He could do nothing more than a humorous poem. One could not even write a meaningful hymn about prayer and worship unless in the prayer and worship one had also shared much that lay behind and beyond the prayer and worship as such.

There will never be a widespread ministry of the laity until the church changes its direction, turns from its preoccupation with self to a concern for the world, offering itself as a servant, an instrument through which God's love and justice and mercy may become operative and visible in the world. This will not happen except as the church is effectively being renewed; for God is calling the church, and each of its members, to be the minister of his purpose in the world. This will mean many changes for the church—changes in attitude, structure, procedure. Above all, it will mean a change in its willingness to take risks and to make sacrifices—new wine in new wineskins! All who love the church and appreciate what it has to give will work for change in all aspects of its life.

One possibility is open to every man, woman, and child. Say Yes to the call. Accept your freedom and the immeasurable riches of God. Open your eyes to see where you have been sent. Be a mature man.

Begin where you are. You may get help from a clergyman (and just your asking may be of the greatest help to *him*). You may find others ready to begin, others who are on the way. Your wife or husband, your son or daughter, may be the only one who is available to start or continue the journey with you. You may have to go it alone as far as the Christian fellowship is concerned. Almost certainly, you will find men and women doing God's work in the world even though they are not conscious of whom they serve. And you are surrounded by a great cloud of witnesses, many of whom have written books or letters, have had books written about them, or both. The Bible is full of such witnesses who tried to fulfill their ministry in a multitude of varied times, places, and circumstances. There are more recent witnesses, such as Dietrich Bonhoeffer, Evelyn Underhill, and Florence Allshorn. There are men and women still very much alive who have written of attempts to be conformed to Christ. Each person will have to find the ones who speak most clearly and strongly to him. In this respect, there is no one who is left without companionship on the way.

Waste no time searching for the uniqueness of the Christian faith. Only Jesus Christ is unique, and each person's uniqueness is found in being conformed to him. Certainly there is nothing unique in the elements of Christian style discussed above. Even such component parts of discipline as prayer, worship, and Scripture-reading are found in a hundred places outside the church. The uniqueness of the Christian faith is the way in which these are combined in Jesus Christ to give the true image of a mature man and the way in which God in Christ has made it possible for men to become mature. Uniqueness is not to be found as one might search for the only lamp of its kind to put in one's picture window, nor can it be designed like a new uniform for the Army. Uniqueness that is sought is always, in the last analysis, little more than a bizarre hat, a mannerism, or a new set of rules. In Christ each man is the unique person God intends him to be. God calls men into the church in order that they may grow as persons in all areas of their lives. Although each man is called to work out his own salvation in fear and trembling, the uniqueness of each person is not discovered or achieved by himself; it is given by God as a man is conformed to Jesus Christ.

By the same token, conformation to Jesus Christ cannot be achieved by obeying law. A Christian style of life does not provide rules by which one becomes conformed. Style is a highly personal matter, achieved with the help of many people; the way in which component parts are fitted together in you. It is a Christian style because it is the way you appear in Jesus Christ. One woman looks stylish in a combination that would make another appear ridiculous. Real style judged by any but the most fatuous standards is far more than a matter of figure. A woman who looks much more like an eraser than a pencil can have more style than the most popular model, and no one else could duplicate the combination of many qualities through which she achieves, and has been given, style.

"A Christian style of life" points in a direction. It is not a law. It indicates the way one has to go when one seeks to encounter God, to enter into a dialogue with him, for encounter and dialogue with God and man is the true end of all men. But the place of encounter, the subject of dialogue, is often so abstracted as to be meaningless for those who live in the world. If you would encounter God and your fellow man (for the two go together), if you would enter into meaningful dialogue with God and man, accept what God has done for you—affirm life, be aware, be responsible, share Christ's sufferings, and be secretly disciplined. In other words, trust and obey: have faith.

During World War II, a young R.A.F. pilot said to a Christian: "Don't try to help me or preach to me or tell me what I ought to think yet. Don't work for my salvation, show me yours, show me it is possible, and the knowledge that something works will give me courage and belief in mine." The young pilot had reached exactly the same point as Eliza Doolittle in the second act of *My Fair Lady:* "If you're on fire, *show* me!" As far as the church is concerned, the world is waiting to be *shown.*

The church is full of men and women who are pious, religious, busy, learned, courteous, attractive. The world is full of exactly the same kind of people. The church talks a great deal about God, but the world cannot see that he makes any difference. The church has exhausted the possibilities of propaganda. In the process, it has cheapened such words as preaching, mission, and gospel to the point where they are almost meaningless. If you doubt this, spend a Sunday listening to "religious broadcasts" sponsored both by the established denominations and by fringe sects. If you don't find yourself screaming: "Words, words, words. I'm so sick of words. . . . Show me!"—well, you can listen again the following Sunday and have your reward.

What both the church and the world need—and at the moment the church needs it more than the world—is to be shown. God needs men who have heard the call, who are aware that they are free, who accept their freedom and the other riches God has bestowed, who recognize that God has sent them to the place where they are and to the people around them. God needs men who trust and obey, who believe and respond. The Bible is the record of what God has done, of the lengths to which he has gone, of the price he has paid, that there may be such men in the world.

It seems fitting to close with the words of someone who was such a man. On the day after the attempt on Hitler's life had failed and Dietrich Bonhoeffer was reasonably certain that he would be executed for his part in the resistance, he wrote from prison to a friend:

> During the last year or so I have come to appreciate the "worldliness" of Christianity as never before. The Christian is not a *homo religiosus,* but a man, pure and simple, just as Jesus was man, compared with John the Baptist anyhow. I don't mean the shallow this-worldliness of the enlightened, of the busy, the comfortable or the lascivious. It's something much more profound than that, something in which the knowledge of death and resurrection is ever present. . . .
>
> Later I discovered and am still discovering up to this very moment that it is only by living completely in this world that one learns to believe. One must abandon every attempt to make something of oneself, whether it be a saint, a converted sinner, churchman (the priestly type, so-called!), a righteous man or an unrighteous one, a sick man or a healthy one. This is what I mean by worldliness—taking life in one's stride, with all its duties and problems, its successes and failures, its experiences and helplessness. It is in such a life that we throw

ourselves utterly in the arms of God and participate in his sufferings in the world and watch with Christ in Gethsemane. That is faith, . . . and that is what makes a man and a Christian. . . . How can success make us arrogant or failure lead us astray, when we participate in the sufferings of God by living in this world?

REFERENCES

In writing of Biblical words throughout the book, I have relied heavily on *A Theological Word Book of the Bible*, edited by Alan Richardson (The Macmillan Company, 1951), and, to a lesser degree, on *A Companion to the Bible*, edited by J. J. von Allmen (Oxford University Press, 1958).

In Chapter II and elsewhere, I have also drawn on Alan Richardson's *The Biblical Doctrine of Work* (S.C.M. Press, Ltd., London, 1952), and L. S. Thornton's *The Common Life in the Body of Christ* (The Dacre Press, 1941).

Reference has also been made to the following books and periodicals in the order listed:

Introduction

"The Ministry of the Laity," faculty paper read on Alumni Day of the Episcopal Theological School, February 1, 1945, by Prof. Joseph F. Fletcher; this was the first time I heard the term. The paper is still an excellent, brief exposition of the subject.

"Findings and Decisions," First Assembly of the World Council of Churches at Amsterdam, Report of Committee IV, Sub-Committee C.

Margaret Parton, "Whither Thou Goest," in *Ladies' Home Journal* (June, 1959).

Mary Louise Villaret, "I Wanted to Be a Lawyer, but . . . ," in *Forth,* Episcopal monthly magazine (September, 1957).

George Parker, "The Time to Pray Is Now," in *Church News*, diocesan paper of the Episcopal Diocese of Pennsylvania (August 19, 1959).

E. Caulfield, letter in the diocesan paper of the Diocese of Qu'Appelle, in Saskatoon, Canada (July, 1959).

Max Picard, *Hitler in Ourselves* (Henry Regnery Company, 1947), p. 51.

Chapter I. You Are a Minister

Hendrik Kraemer, *A Theology of the Laity* (The Westminster Press, 1958), p. 136.

William Temple, *Social Witness and Evangelism* (The Epworth Press, 1943), p. 17.

From a poem attributed to "a pastor in Essen" by Karl Barth, in the Preface to the Fifth Edition of *The Epistle to the Romans* (Oxford University Press).

Chapter II. You Are Called

Suzanne de Dietrich: "A message from a community to a community." See Foreword for my debt to Mlle. de Dietrich.

Chapter III. You Are Free

John P. Marquand, *Sincerely, Willis Wayde* (Little, Brown & Co., 1955).

Chapter IV. You Are Sent

Hendrik Kraemer, *op. cit.*, p. 131.

Chapter V. You Are Rich!

L. S. Thornton, *op. cit.*, p. 74.

Chapter VI. A Christian Style of Life

The Book of Common Prayer, p. 588.

Dietrich Bonhoeffer, *The Cost of Discipleship*, tr. by R. H. Fuller (The Macmillan Company, 1949), p. 56.

Dietrich Bonhoeffer, *Prisoner for God*, tr. by R. H. Fuller (The Macmillan Company, 1953), p. 166.

Dietrich Bonhoeffer, *Ethics*, tr. by N. H. Smith (S.C.M. Press, Ltd., London, 1955), p. 22.

Jacques Ellul, *The Presence of the Kingdom*, tr. by Olive Wyon (The Westminster Press, 1952), pp. 146 f.

Jean Pierre de Caussade, *Self-abandonment to Divine Providence*, tr. by Algar Thorald (Burns Oates & Washbourne, Ltd., London, 1959), p. 16.

Ellul, *op. cit.*, p. 147.

Chapter VII. Affirmation

J. H. Oldham, *Real Life Is Meeting*, Christian News Letter Books (The Seabury Press, Inc., 1953).

Evelyn Underhill, *Collected Papers*, ed. by Lucy Menzies (Longmans, Green & Co., Inc., 1946), p. 216.

Charles Williams, *Greater Trumps* (Pellegrini & Cudahy, 1950), p. 143.

Alex Miller, *Renewal of Man* (Doubleday & Co., Inc., 1955), p. 54.
Millard Lampell, in the article "The Human Spirit Behind 'The Wall,'" by Seymour Peck in *The New York Times* (October 9, 1960).

Chapter VIII. Awareness

Evelyn Underhill, *op. cit.*, p. 185.
Rudolf Bultmann, "Theology for Freedom and Responsibility," *The Christian Century* (August 27, 1958).
Vincent Sheean, *Personal History* (Modern Library, 1940), p. 427.
Suzanne de Dietrich, *God's Unfolding Purpose* (The Westminster Press, 1960). This is, in my opinion, the best book for a serious study of the whole Bible, and the only one that does not tend to get between the reader and the Bible. This is also true of her other books, *Free Men* and *The Witnessing Community* (both published by The Westminster Press, 1961 and 1958).

Chapter IX. Responsibility

Dietrich Bonhoeffer, *Ethics*, p. 77, and again, p. 226.
John C. Bennett, "Faith and Responsibility," in *The Christian Century* (December 3, 1958).
Erich Fromm, *The Art of Loving* (Harper & Brothers, 1956), p. 28.
Dietrich Bonhoeffer, *The Cost of Discipleship*, p. 101.
Gibson Winter, *Love and Conflict* (Doubleday & Co., Inc., 1958), p. 36.
The quotation, "The missileman will be . . . ," is from "Pilots, Missilemen, and Robots," by Paul Jacobs, *The Reporter* (February 6, 1958).

Chapter X. Sharing Christ's Sufferings

Charles Gore, Henry L. Goudge, Alfred Guillaume, eds., *A New Commentary on Holy Scripture* (The Macmillan Company, 1936).

Chapter XI. Secret Discipline

Gabriel Marcel, *Etre et Avoir*, p. 106, quoted in J. H. Oldham, *Life Is Commitment* (Harper & Brothers, 1952), p. 99.

Conclusion

Dietrich Bonhoeffer, *Prisoner for God*, p. 123.
William Temple, *Hope of a New World* (The Macmillan Company, 1941), p. 70.
Ronald Gregor Smith, *The New Man* (Harper & Brothers, 1956), p. 82.
The story of the R.A.F. pilot, *The Notebooks of Florence Allshorn* (S.C.M. Press, Ltd., London, 1957), p. 15.
Lerner and Loewe, *My Fair Lady,* a musical play (Coward-McCann, Inc., 1956).
Dietrich Bonhoeffer, *Prisoner for God*, pp. 168 f.